# SALVATION TO GENTILES

# WILD OLIVE BRANCHES AND GOOD OLIVE TREE

# LESLIE M. JOHN

Leslie M. John

# SALVATION TO GENTILES

# WILD OLIVE BRANCHES AND GOOD OLIVE TREE

## LESLIE M. JOHN

My writings are deposited with Library of Congress Copyright Office, 101 Independence Avenue, SE Washington, DC 20559-6000, USA, and certificates obtained. All Scriptures in electronic format are from King James Version (KJV) from Open domain.

This book in print media is a compilation of extracts from my e-books "Predestination", "Hosea Marries Gomer", "The Church and The Kingdom", "Death Defeated", "The Sojourners" and with great deal of new text added to them to maintain connectivity and flow of thoughts.

ISBN-10: 0989028372

ISBN-13: 978-0-9890283-7-0

Leslie M. John

Leslie M. John

Leslie M. John

**Table of Contents**

Leslie M. John

Leslie M. John

Leslie M. John

Leslie M. John

Leslie M. John

Leslie M. John

Leslie M. John

# PREFACE

I. My mission is to proclaim the good news of our Lord Jesus Christ as revealed to me through Holy Bible and from various teachers, preachers, and commentators. This is my voluntary service to God in the name of His only begotten Son Lord Jesus Christ. I share the truth of knowledge of God with others with good intention of bringing them to the knowledge of the living God, the God of Abraham, the God of Isaac, the God of Jacob, and the Father of our Lord Jesus Christ.

III. There are fundamental truths which I will not compromise upon. Explanations, on which Christians dispute among themselves, are secondary to the fundamental truths that I believe in. My mission is not to convert anyone to Christianity or make any attempt in the direction of forcible conversions. One may accept or reject any or part of my teachings.

IV. I firmly believe in the saying of Jesus, who said:

"No man can come to me, except the Father which hath sent me draw him: and I will raise him up at the last day" John 6:44. My efforts to teach or preach are of no use unless Jesus Himself intervenes and the Father draws a person unto Jesus

Leslie M. John

Leslie M. John

# INTRODUCTION

**A**postle Paul explains in Romans 11th Chapter elaborately God's provisions and His plan for the salvation of Gentiles. He writes that it was not because of Israel's stumbling or because they were stumbling blocks to anybody that their eyes were blinded and their ears were hard on hearing but because they fell short of understanding Lord Jesus Christ as their Messiah. They believed in doing good works for their salvation and  recompense God for what He did for them.   It is because of their misunderstanding, and rejection of Lord Jesus Christ as their Messiah that salvation is come unto the Gentiles.

Psalmist writes..."What shall I render unto the LORD for all his benefits toward me? I will take the cup of salvation, and call upon the name of the LORD" Psalms 116:12-13. The Lord says..."If I were hungry, I would not tell thee: for the world is mine, and the fulness thereof. Will I eat the flesh of bulls, or drink the blood of goats? Psalms 50:12-13

Paul warns Gentiles that they are like branches of wild olive tree grafted into the places where the branches of the natural olive tree existed.  The branches of natural olive tree were cut off in order that Gentiles are made partakers of the root and fatness of the natural olive tree. Paul, therefore, says, Gentiles should not be of high-minded, but fear God. The branches of the natural olive tree were broken off by God because of their unbelief, and the Gentiles, who were like branches of wild olive tree, have blessings of Abraham, now, after grafting them into good olive tree. The sap and blessings from the root of the natural olive tree flowed into the wild olive branches.. If Gentiles were to be high-minded and take pride in themselves or their own merits, God will not hesitate to chastise them. If God did not spare the natural branches of the olive tree would He tolerate the grafted olive branches?  Never!

Leslie M. John

# INTRODUCTION

Leslie M. John

# CHAPTER 1
# PETER'S MESSAGE

**W**hen Peter spoke of Jesus of Nazareth that He was a man approved of God, he had full knowledge of Jesus, because Peter was a disciple of Jesus Christ. Peter knew that Mary was the earthly mother of Jesus and Joseph had purposed earlier to put her off when Joseph came to know that Mary was pregnant. Jesus was born of the Virgin Mary of the Holy Spirit (Matthew 1:20).

Later in his life Peter wrote in his 1 epistle Chapter 1 a great message honoring "God the Father of our Lord Jesus Christ, who has begotten us unto a lively hope by the resurrection of Jesus Christ from the dead to an inheritance, and undefiled, and that fades not, which is reserved for us". (1 Peter 1:3-5)

This Peter, an Apostle of Jesus Christ said in Acts 2:21-24 that whosoever shall call on the name of the Lord shall be saved. This Peter addressed the men in Israel and testified about Jesus of Nazareth that he was approved of God and did miracles and wonders and signs. Peter said that they took Jesus, who was delivered by the determinate counsel of foreknowledge of God, and killed him and that God raised Him from the pains of death, which could not hold him Jesus ascended into heaven and seated on the right hand of the Father and will come back after all his enemies are brought to His footstool. (Acts 2:21-25, 31, Psalm 16:8-11). Peter also quoted the David and his prophecy about Jesus Christ. (Psalm 110:1)

Before Peter went to meet Cornelius, an uncircumcised Gentile, a devout man, who feared God and gave much alms, and also prayed to God always, God taught a lesson to Peter. It was when Peter was still thinking about Mosaic Law and ordinances. Even though he was hungry he had determination not to eat that which was forbidden under Mosaic Law and Ordinances. Jesus had already ascended into heaven by this time, and the Apostles had already begun preaching the Gospel of grace. It was not the kingdom message that they were preaching, but the Gospel

Leslie M. John

of Grace. The message was that Jesus was crucified by sinful people like me, and that he died for saving the sinner, and that he was buried and rose on the third day from the dead and after forty days ascended into heaven. Peter was the first one to preach about this fact as we read in Acts Chapter 2.

Later in Acts Chapter 9 there is narration of how Paul, who persecuted Christians, was encountered by Jesus, who said that He was the one whom Paul was persecuting. When Christians are persecuted Jesus felt that he was being persecuted.

It was this Lord Jesus Christ, the Son of God, the very God himself, who said to Peter to go to Cornelius to give him the salvation message. Before going to Cornelius, Peter saw a man named "Aeneas" sick of palsy at Lydda. Peter said to him "...Jesus Christ maketh thee whole: arise, and make thy bed. And he arose immediately" (Acts 9:34). Because of this miracle done by Peter in the name of Jesus, many turned to the Lord. Later Peter prayed and raised Tabitha (also known as Dorcas) from the dead. Many believed in the Lord.

## PETER STAYS IN THE HOUSE OF TANNER

Then Peter went to Simon, who was a tanner, and stayed with him for many days. Peter did not have any hesitation to stay in the house of the tanner for many days.

"And it came to pass, that he tarried many days in Joppa with one Simon a tanner". (Acts 9:43)

## CORNELIUS' VISION

Cornelius saw an angel of God in a vision saying to him that his prayers and his alms to people were honored by God. The angel of God said to Cornelius that he should send word for Simon Peter (the disciple of Lord Jesus Christ), who stayed in the house of one named Simon, who was a tanner. Cornelius sent two of his servants to Joppa to call for Simon Peter. (Acts 10:1-8)

# TANNER

A 'tanner' is the one who deals with dead animals. International Standard Bible Encyclopedia describes 'Tanner' as:

Quote: "tan'-er (burseus, from bursa "a hide"): The only references to a tanner are in Ac 9:43; 10:6, 32. The Jews looked upon tanning as an undesirable occupation and well they might, for at best it was accompanied with unpleasant odors and unattractive sights, if not even ceremonially unclean. We can imagine that Simon the tanner found among the disciples of Jesus a fellowship which had been denied him before. Peter made the way still easier for Simon by choosing his house as his abode while staying in Joppa. Simon's house was by the seashore, as is true of the tanneries along the Syrian coast today, so that the foul-smelling liquors from the vats can be drawn off with the least nuisance, and so that the salt water may be easily accessible for washing the skins during the tanning process.

These tanneries are very unpretentious affairs, usually consisting of one or two small rooms and a courtyard. Within are the vats made either of stone masonry, plastered within and without, or cut out of the solid rock. The sheep or goat skins are smeared on the flesh side with a paste of slaked lime and then folded up and allowed to stand until the hair loosens. The hair and fleshy matter are removed, the skins are plumped in lime, bated in a concoction first of dog dung and afterward in one of fermenting bran, in much the same way as in a modern tannery. The bated skins are tanned in sumach (Arabic summak), which is the common tanning material in Syria and Palestine.

After drying, the leather is blackened on one side by rubbing on a solution made by boiling vinegar with old nails or pieces of copper, and the skin is finally given a dressing of olive oil. In the more modern tanneries degras is being imported for the currying processes. For dyeing the rams' skins red (Ex 25:1-40) they rub on a solution of qermes (similar to cochineal; see DYEING ), dry, oil, and polish with a smooth stone" Unquote.

Leslie M. John

Bible emphasizes Peter's stay in the house of a tanner: When Bible mentions specifically an incidence it is not without any significance. It needs serious consideration.

"And it came to pass, that he tarried many days in Joppa with one Simon a tanner". (Acts 9:43)

"He lodgeth with one Simon a tanner, whose house is by the sea side: he shall tell thee what thou oughtest to do". (Acts 10:6)

It was one just before Peter spoke to Cornelius, who was a Roman uncircumcised Gentile from Italian Band. Cornelius was baptized later. Points to note Tanning is unclean. Tanner is unclean. Gentiles were unclean in the sight of Jews. Yet God said what he called as 'clean' man should not call it as 'unclean'.

Hebrew Strong's Number 2931 is "tame' " transliterated as "taw-may' "

In KJV the word "Unclean" is mentioned as defiled , 5; infamous, 1; polluted, 1; pollution, 1; unclean, 79

Greek Strong's number 169 transliterated as "Akathartos" is found in KJV as

KJV (30) - foul, 2; unclean, 28;

"Or if a soul touch any unclean thing, whether it be a carcase of an unclean beast, or a carcase of unclean cattle, or the carcase of unclean creeping things, and if it be hidden from him; he also shall be unclean, and guilty". Leviticus 5:2  and also there  are more details about dietary restrictions imposed on the children of Israel. These instructions included that they shall eat the beasts that have  parted hoof,   cloven-footed and Chew the cud.

But they shall not eat

Leslie M. John

Camel because he chews the cud, but has no divided hoof

Coney because he chews the cud, but has no divided hoof

Hare because he chews the cud, but has no divided hoof

Swine because he chews the cud, but has no divided hoof

God said the children of Israel shall not eat their flesh and they shall not touch their carcasses. They are all considered as 'Unclean" by God. (Leviticus 11:2-8)

PETER'S VISION

On the morrow when the servants of Cornelius were reaching the city, Peter went upon the housetop to pray. It was about sixth hour and Peter was very hungry. Before he went to eat with Tanner, he saw a vision. In the vision he saw heaven opened and a certain vessel descending towards him. It was like a great sheet knit at the four corners and let down to the earth. The sheet contained variety of animals; four-footed beasts, wild beasts, creeping things and fowls of the air. Peter heard a voice saying to him to rise, kill and eat. But Peter refused to eat because there were animals that were prohibited to be eaten as per Mosaic Law and ordinances. Peter said that he had never eaten that which is common or unclean. The voice said to him second time, and Peter refused to eat. The voice said to Peter that what God had cleansed should not be called common by him. This was done three times and the sheet was retrieved into heaven. (Acts 10:10-16)

# PETER MEETS CORNELIUS

While Peter was in trance and thought on the vision, the Spirit spoke to him and said to him that three men were seeking him. Peter was asked to arise and go with them without doubting. Peter obeyed the voice and went with the men to Cornelius and said that he was Peter. Just before Peter identified himself Cornelius fell on the feet of Peter and worshipped him; but Peter lifted him and said that he was also a man. He meant that God is the only One who is to be worshipped and none else. Peter saw in the home of Cornelius many others who were there to listen

Leslie M. John

to him. Peter, who was a Jew, asked

Cornelius, who was an un-circumcised Gentile, as to why he sent word for him knowing fully well that it was unlawful for Jew to keep company with Gentile. Cornelius said to Peter that he saw a man in bright clothing stood before him four days ago when he was fasting and said to him that his prayers were honored and his alms were recognized by God. Cornelius continued saying that the man, whom he saw, asked him to send word for Peter, specifically mentioning the name as Simon, whose name was Peter, and who was staying with a 'tanner'. That is the reason why he called for him and said that they were all there to hear what God had to say to all of them in his house.

Leslie M. John

# CHAPTER 2
# SALVATION TO GENTILES

The brethren at Puteoli who heard of Paul and others went to meet them at cities called 'Appii forum' and 'The three taverns'. Paul thanked God because he was very near to Rome and he took courage. On their arrival at Rome the Centurion delivered the prisoners to the captain guard but the Centurion with the help of a soldier took care of Paul. (Acts 28:15-16)

It was Paul's opportunity, then, to speak to the Christians at Rome and defend his position. Paul spoke to the men and brethren at Rome that he was innocent of the charges that were leveled against him. He did neither mislead nor did work against the customs of the fathers, yet he was imprisoned and brought from Jerusalem to Rome to stand before Caesar. Earlier he was examined of the charges leveled against him and they found that he did nothing that deserved death penalty. Jews laid grievous complaints against Paul, but they could not prove. But when Jews spoke against him he was constrained to appeal to Caesar. Festus, willing to show favor to Jews asked Paul if he would like to go to Jerusalem for trial but Paul asked that he may be sent to stand at Caesar's judgment seat.(Acts 25:7-12)

Paul was a Roman citizen, a Pharisee, Hebrew of Hebrews, a Jew by birth of the tribe of Benjamin (Philippians 3:5). Earlier Paul was arrested at Jerusalem because he was proclaiming that Jesus was the Son of God. Jews thought Paul was speaking blasphemy. Paul also taught that circumcision was not required for salvation. Jews took serious exceptions to his teachings. Paul was held prisoner for two years at Caesarea.

"But after two years Porcius Festus came into Felix' room: and Felix, willing to shew the Jews a pleasure, left Paul bound." (Acts 24:27)

Paul did not mean to offend Jews nor accuse them because of their false allegations leading to his apprehension but he was defending himself

Leslie M. John

that he did nothing that deserved punishment. At Rome Paul called Jews to let them know of these facts.

Paul's speech was filled with hope for the disturbed Israel and said that he was bound in chains for this reason. But when they heard of Paul's speech they said that they did not receive any letter from Judea or heard any word about Paul from any of the brethren. Yet, they desired to hear from Paul about the entire situation and about the Jews of whom there was a bad talk all over.

The Jews there set apart a day for Paul to speak and expound of the matters that were of much concern to them and their sect. This was obviously very interesting situation and many gathered to listen to Paul. Making use of the opportunity he was given, Paul spoke elaborately about Jesus from out of the Law of Moses, and out of the prophets from morning till evening. As it usually happens everywhere, even now, some believed Paul's exposition and some did not believe. The Jews did not agree with one another among themselves and some of them did not believe what Paul spoke of Jesus.

Seeing that many Jews leaving the place where he was speaking about Jesus, he reminded of the prophesy that Isaiah spoke to the fathers that "Hearing ye shall hear, and shall not understand; and seeing ye shall see, and not perceive: For the heart of this people is waxed gross, and their ears are dull of hearing, and their eyes have they closed; lest they should see with their eyes, and hear with their ears, and understand with their heart, and should be converted, and I should heal them" Acts 28:26,27

The prophesy was in Isaiah 6:9-10 which reads as "And he said, Go, and tell this people, Hear ye indeed, but understand not; and see ye indeed, but perceive not. Make the heart of this people fat, and make their ears heavy, and shut their eyes; lest they see with their eyes, and hear with their ears, and understand with their heart, and convert, and be healed"

Lord Jesus Christ quoted this prophesy earlier to Jews as we read in Matthew 13:14

Leslie M. John

" And in them is fulfilled the prophecy of Esaias, which saith, By hearing ye shall hear, and shall not understand; and seeing ye shall see, and shall not perceive"

"But though he had done so many miracles before them, yet they believed not on him: That the saying of Esaias the prophet might be fulfilled, which he spake, Lord, who hath believed our report? and to whom hath the arm of the Lord been revealed? Therefore they could not believe, because that Esaias said again, He hath blinded their eyes, and hardened their heart; that they should not see with their eyes, nor understand with their heart, and be converted, and I should heal them" (John 12:37-40)

Paul was upset at this point of time and said that the "salvation of God is sent unto the Gentiles, and they will hear it".

The Jews departed and reasoned among themselves. Paul was at Rome for two whole years in his hired house, and spoke of the kingdom of God to all those who visited him at his home. He taught them about Lord Jesus Christ with boldness and no man forbad him from speaking about Jesus.

Acts Chapter 28 or any other scripture does not give more details of Paul's ministry afterwards or as to what happened to his life. Secular history says that he died as a martyr for Christ.
There are few points that need our attention here. When Paul said that salvation of God was sent to the Gentiles was it the first time that Gentiles heard of Lord Jesus Christ either from others or from Paul? No, Peter spoke of Lord Jesus Christ to Cornelius as we read in Acts Chapter 10. Was Cornelius Jew or Circumcised? No, Cornelius was not a Jew and he was not circumcised to be considered as a Proselyte. Was he grafted into Jews based on Paul's exposition that we read in Romans Chapter 11 Yes, but his grafting into the Natural branches was not anything special or of more importance than any other Gentile! All Gentiles who are considered as grafted based on the exposition of Romans Chapter 11 are just as equal in status as we are as "One New Man" as Cornelius was. Nothing in the scriptures suggests that the grafting of Gentiles in Acts period was of extra importance or of less importance than that of those

Leslie M. John

Gentiles who are saved after the Acts period.

"And when he had found him, he brought him unto Antioch. And it came to pass, that a whole year they assembled themselves with the church, and taught much people. And the disciples were called Christians first in Antioch. " (Acts 11:26)

When Jews rejected Paul's preaching as we read in Acts Chapter 13 the Gentiles requested him that the word of God may be preached to them. On the next Sabbath Paul spoke to the Gentiles and they heard the word of God. Jews took objection to Paul's preaching but Paul and Barnabas were bold enough to speak about Jesus and that led to Jews getting envy of Paul and contradicted him. When there was a difference of opinion among Jews and religious proselytes Paul and Barnabas spoke to them and persuaded them to continue in the grace of God (Acts 13:43).

 Paul said to them that it was necessary that the word of God be spoken to them first and then to Gentiles and he did that exactly as Jesus commanded him to do. Some say that all these Gentiles saved during the Acts period were the descendants of Jacob, but there is no convincing evidence to show that they were all descendants of Jacob.

"For so hath the Lord commanded us, saying, I have set thee to be a light of the Gentiles, that thou shouldest be for salvation unto the ends of the earth." (Acts 13:47)

Earlier, Jesus had compassion on Centurion as we read in Matthew Chapter 8, and on Canaanite woman as we read in Matthew Chapter 15. No doubt Jesus came to seek the lost sheep of Israel but his coming was not with absolute negligence toward Gentiles. Jesus resisted his disciples going in the way of Gentiles as we read in Matthew Chapter 10, yet his concern for Gentiles was not with absolute negligence toward them, otherwise, the most familiar verse John 3:16 would have been of no consequence.

 "For God so loved the world, that he gave his only begotten Son, that whosoever believeth in him should not perish, but have everlasting life". (John 3:16)

Leslie M. John

# GENTILES SHALL SEE
# HIS RIGHTEOUSNESS

"And the Gentiles shall see thy righteousness, and all kings thy glory: and thou shalt be called by a new name, which the mouth of the LORD shall name" (Isaiah 62:2)

Lord Jesus Christ, who is the messiah, says that He will not sit quite, nor will He rest until He redeems the city of Jerusalem. He has set watchmen upon the walls of Jerusalem and they will not keep quite nor will sleep but keep a watch over the city and will make the city a praise of the earth. This is a promise of Messiah and He has sworn by His right hand and by the arm of His strength. He promised that none of the enemies of Jerusalem will eat its corn as their food no stranger will ever drink its wine. Gentiles will see its righteousness.

Lord Jesus Christ defeats the kings loyal to Antichrist at 'Armageddon', and sits on the throne of David and reigns for a thousand years. In the thousand years of His rule there shall be perfect peace. Satan will be bound with chains and thrown into abyss by an angel who comes from heaven. Later Satan will be released for a short time when he goes Gog and Magog to deceive the nations but fire from God comes down from heaven and devours Satan. (Revelation Ch. 20:8)

The dead who did not accept Jesus Christ as their personal savior will resurrect at that time. The Lord shall judge them at the 'Great white throne' and cast them along with death, hell, and the devil and his angels into the 'lake of fire' to be tormented for ever and ever. This is the second death. For those who are saved, there is no second death but they will have everlasting life to be with the Lord for ever and ever. Note here when Antichrist and false prophet are thrown into the lake of fire! It is before the devil that deceived!!! Revelation 20:10 confirms it.

When the devil was cast into the lake of fire, the Antichrist and the false prophet were already there in the lake of fire. These are only the ones who will be in the lake of fire before the 'Great White Throne Judgment' (Revelation 16:16 and Revelation 20:8-10). Does the Scripture say any

Leslie M. John

body is thrown into the lake of fire before Antichrist and false prophet. No, not at all!

There shall come out of heaven a New Jerusalem and we, who are saved, shall be in that Holy City. The Church is the bride of our Lord Jesus Christ and will be with Him for ever and ever reigning along with Him and every individual having been conformed to His image, irrespective of their earthly affiliation, while they were on the earth, to Jews or Gentiles.

Leslie M. John

# SALVATION FOR THOSE WHO BELIEVE IN JESUS

"Now therefore ye are no more strangers and foreigners, but fellow citizens with the saints, and of the household of God; And are built upon the foundation of the apostles and prophets, Jesus Christ himself being the chief corner stone" (Ephesians 2:19-20)

For as the body is one, and hath many members, and all the members of that one body, being many, are one body: so also is Christ. For by one Spirit are we all baptized into one body, whether we be Jews or Gentiles, whether we be bond or free; and have been all made to drink into one Spirit. For the body is not one member, but many (1 Corinthians 12:12-14)

Apostle Paul was the one who was sent out to preach the Gospel of Jesus Christ to the Gentiles. The salvation is by grace alone through faith in Jesus. Paul said circumcision is not required to be observed. Baptism is not part of salvation. Peter preached baptism as part of salvation but Paul did not preach baptism as part of salvation. There were so much of legalism in Peter's preaching, but in Paul's preaching "Grace" is emphasized upon.

This is not to say that they disagreed upon what they agreed upon to preach or preached different Gospels, but Peter basically was preaching in early days only to Jews while Paul preached to Gentiles.

Did Paul rebuke Peter? Yes, he did. (Galatians 2:7-8). Did Peter retort Paul? No. Peter supported Paul at Jerusalem Council. (Acts 15:7). Was Peter preaching a heresy? No. Their preaching differed because they preached at different periods of time. Paul was not even converted when Peter preached (Acts 2;38)

Notice the words, "our", "we", "all", "everyone" in Isaiah 53:4-6. These words include Jews and Gentiles all alike. Jesus came into this world for His own people, but His own rejected Him and the salvation has gone out even to the Gentiles. His death was not exclusively for a group of people but for all. Whosoever believes in Lord Jesus Christ as Savior shall

Leslie M. John

not perish but have everlasting life. Those who reject Him as Savior will surely perish. It is they who will be judged at the "Great White Throne" (Revelation 20:11-15)

"Surely he hath borne our griefs, and carried our sorrows: yet we did esteem him stricken, smitten of God, and afflicted. But he [was] wounded for our transgressions, [he was] bruised for our iniquities: the chastisement of our peace [was] upon him; and with his stripes we are healed. All we like sheep have gone astray; we have turned everyone to his own way; and the LORD hath laid on him the iniquity of us all" Isaiah 53:4-6

# A LIGHT TO LIGHTEN GENTILES

Joseph and Mary offered a pair of turtle doves as sacrifice. Because they were considerably poor they could not offer a lamb as burnt offering but as an alternative as the provisions of Law permitted they offered turtle doves. (Cf. Leviticus 12:1-6)

Simeon saw the child Jesus and took him in his arms and blessed God and prayed that now that he saw the savior of the Gentiles he may be allowed departing in peace. Simeon's testimony was great in that he said that he saw the salvation in Jesus and Jesus was the one whom the Father had prepared before the face of all the people and also that Jesus was the light to lighten the Gentiles, and the glory of His people Israel.

"A light to lighten the Gentiles, and the glory of thy people Israel" (Luke 2:32)

Joseph and Mary marveled when Simeon spoke those words. Simeon blessed them and said to them that Jesus was set for the fall of, and for the rising again of, many in Israel and for a sign which shall be spoken of. Simeon forewarned Mary that Jesus will suffer and his death shall put her to much grief. That was a forewarning for her to be prepared to see the death of Jesus in future.

Before the birth of Jesus Elizabeth, the mother of John the Baptist said:

"And whence is this to me, that the mother of my Lord should come to me?" (Luke 1:43)

"And Mary said, My soul doth magnify the Lord, And my spirit hath rejoiced in God my Saviour". (Luke 1:46-47)

Lord Jesus Christ was the Savior of Elizabeth and Mary. He is our Savior and salvation belongs to him. Whoever accepts Jesus as his/her Lord will be saved.

## APOSTLE PAUL TURNS TO GENTILES

The message Paul spoke on different occasions before he finally settled to speak to the Gentiles was about Salvation which is free gift and is not associated with law and works. The message Peter spoke initially was about the "kingdom of God" to Jews before he spoke to Gentiles. The Kingdom, which was originally supposed to come into existence, provided Jews accepted Jesus as their Messiah was postponed to accommodate Gentiles in the Church.

Jews rejected Jesus as their Messiah and this eventually paved the way for Gentiles to come into the Church. But then, was this a happening without the knowledge of God? No, God had salvation to Gentiles in his plan and deliberately blinded the eyes of Jews. (Romans Chapters.9-11)

God sent His one and only Son Jesus Christ into this world to redeem mankind from the bondage of sin. Jesus, who was without any sin, bore our sin on himself (1 Peter 2:24, 2 Corinthians 5:21). He paid the price of our salvation. Whoever accepts this fact and confesses by mouth will receive everlasting life.

The price Lord Jesus Christ paid on the cross for our sake was not silver or gold but his own precious blood. The Scriptures say that silver and gold are perishable and corruptible and will fade away. Lord Jesus did not redeem us from those corruptible things but by his own blood. He is the creator of this universe and all the elements in therein. Who can

Page 31

Leslie M. John

please him with the elements of this world - none.

Acts Chapter 13 has details about Apostle Paul's endeavors to turn Jews from their obstinate stance of rejection of Jesus as their Messiah. He details great many events that have taken place in the past right from the days of Abraham until the resurrection of Jesus. Paul tried to convey the message of salvation that is available only in Lord Jesus Christ but Jews not only stirred up the devout and honorable women and the chief men of the Antioch, but also persecuted Paul and Barnabas. They expelled them from their region. As Lord Jesus Christ commanded his disciples to shake off the dust against that city and go ahead to another city (Matthew 10:14) Paul and Barnabas followed the example and they shook off the dust off their feet against them. The disciples were filled with joy and with the Holy Spirit.
It started when the CHURCH at Antioch had prophets and teachers among who were four names were prominent. They were: (1) Barnabas (2) Simeon who was also called Niger (3) Lucius of Cyrene and (4) Manaen

The Holy Spirit separated Paul and Barnabas for working for Lord Jesus Christ. The Church laid hands on Paul and Barnabas and sent them for work. This was a follow up of what Lord Jesus wanted from Paul. Lord Jesus Christ called Saul and said about him that "...he is a chosen vessel unto me, to bear my name before the Gentiles, and kings, and the children of Israel" (Acts 9:15) Saul was called by the name Paul.

This was the beginning of the ministry by Paul first to the Jews and then to the Gentiles. Earlier Peter spoke to the men of Israel (Ref. Acts Chapters 1 and 2). The early ministry of Paul and Barnabas was not an easy one. They were sent out into the midst of powerful unbelieving men of Israel and then to the Gentiles. The Church and the Ministry was in the beginning stages. As they were traveling from Selucia and from there to Cyprus they encountered many hardships.

One of the tough encounters they faced was with a sorcerer, who was a Jew and a false prophet, whose name was Bar-jesus. After dealing with this sorcerer they had another sorcerer come in their way and his name

Leslie M. John

was Elymas, who opposed preaching of the Gospel of Jesus Christ.

When they were at Salamis they preached the word of God in the SYNAGOGUES of the Jews. Paul and Barnabas had John also with them for working for the Lord. While they were passing through that isle to Paphos, they came across Bar-jesus, who was with the deputy of the country, Sergius Paulus. Sergius was a wise man and he called Paul and Barnabas and desired to hear the word of God from them. Elymas opposed preaching of the word of God to Sergius Paulus thinking that Sergius would turn away from his faith. Paul filled with the Holy Spirit set his eyes on Elymas and said to him...

"O full of all subtilty and all mischief, thou child of the devil, thou enemy of all righteousness, wilt thou not cease to pervert the right ways of the Lord? And now, behold, the hand of the Lord is upon thee, and thou shalt be blind, not seeing the sun for a season" (Acts 13:10)

Elymas lost sight "for a season" because of the curse and seeing this deputy Sergius Paulus believed in the Lord.

From Paphos Paul, Barnabas and John went to Perga in Pemphylia. From there John departed from then and returned to Jerusalem. Paul and Barnabas departed from Perga and came to Antioth in Pisidia and went to SYNAGOGUE on the Sabbath day and sat down. The rulers of the SYNAGOGUE sent unto them to speak if they have anything to speak about the law, prophets.

Paul then stood and addressed them as "Men of Israel, and ye that fear God, give audience."

Paul went on describing in detail as to how God of the people of Israel chose the patriarchs and exalted them when they were as strangers in the land of Egypt. With great might God delivered them from the bondage under Pharaoh.

God destroyed seven nations when they were on their journey from

Leslie M. John

Egypt to Canaan. God gave to them Judges to guide them in the way of the Lord for four hundred and fifty years until Samuel the prophet. But then they desired to have a king to rule over them. God gave Saul the son of Cis, one who was of the tribe of Benjamin, for forty years.

God removed him and raised up unto them David to be their king and the Lord himself said that he found David, the son of Jesse as a man after his own heart and that he will fulfill His will. God raised up from the seed of David a Savior unto Israel and his name was Jesus.

John the Baptist preached the repentance by Baptism to all the people of Israel. John said he was not worthy to lose the latchet of the One who comes after him. Paul says that the salvation was sent out to the men and brethren, children of the stock of Abraham, and whosoever fears God. Every Sabbath day these men of Jerusalem and their rulers who read in the SYNAGOGUES the law and prophet did not yet believe on Jesus but condemned him. They found no reason to kill Jesus, yet they desired of Pilate the Jesus should be slain.

When they had fulfilled everything that was written of him they took him down from the cross and laid in a sepulcher. But God raised him from the dead. Jesus was seen by many during those days and Paul says Paul and his Barnabas were witnesses to these events.

Paul tells the audience that Jesus the Messiah had come as prophesied (Psalm Chapter 2:7) and God raised him from the dead and he will have sure mercies of David. Even as David saw corruption and was laid to rest along with his fathers, no one could see corruption in Jesus. This was also in fulfillment of prophesying as prophesied. (Psalms 16:10)

Paul then declares that through the Son of man was preached the forgiveness of sins. He declares that all those who believe him are justified from all things from which they could not be justified by the law of Moses.

Prophet Habakkuk had burden for the children of Israel that they were going away from the Lord and slack in following the commandments of

Leslie M. John

the Lord. The prophet cries out to God showing his concern for them and says how long these people would go unpunished for their wickedness and iniquity. The Lord says that he would raise up Chaldeans against them and scatter them. God warned about this in earlier as we read in Deuteronomy 28:64-67. As per the word of God they were scattered and God says that he will do the work that they do not believe even if they were told about it. Paul quotes this verse in his speech and warns Jews about their disbelief and rejection of Jesus as their Messiah.

Behold ye among the heathen, and regard, and wonder marvellously: for I will work a work in your days, which ye will not believe, though it be told you. (Habakkuk 1:5)

As prophesied earlier the Jews did neither accept Jesus as their Messiah nor did Apostle Paul as one sent to preach the gospel of Jesus Christ. The Gentiles came in when they saw that Jews left from the SYNAGOGUE and requested Paul and Barnabas to preach to them the same message that they spoke to the Jews the next Sabbath day. Congregation was divided over this issue and may Jews and religious proselyte followed Paul and Barnabas.

Paul and Barnabas advised all of them to continue in the grace of God. Almost the whole city came together to hear the word of God from Paul and Barnabas the next Sabbath day. But the envy in Jews grew more when they saw the multitudes following Paul and Barnabas and spoke against them and said to the multitude that Paul and Barnabas were contradicting and blaspheming. It was then that Paul and Barnabas became bold and said that it was necessary that the word of God should have been first spoken to the Jews and admonished that they were not worthy of everlasting life. It was then that they turned to the Gentiles. It was then that Paul said that he was set apart to take the Gospel of Jesus Christ and the message of salvation to the Gentiles unto the ends of the earth.

When the Gentiles heard these words from Apostle Paul they were glad and glorified the word of the Lord and as many as were elected by God unto eternal life believed. The word of the Lord was published the entire region. When the Jews expelled them they shook off the dust off their

Leslie M. John

feet and went to Iconium. (Acts 13:40-52)

## SIMEON SAW SALVATION IN JESUS

"Then took he him up in his arms, and blessed God, and said, Lord, now lettest thou thy servant depart in peace, according to thy word" (Luke 2:28-29)

That Lord Jesus Christ has come not only for Jews but also for the Gentiles is seen here in Luke Chapter 2:21-35 where description of one named Simeon is given. There are many speculations as to who this Simeon was although there is no record of his genealogy. All that we have is the fact that Simeon was sufficiently old; he was just and devout. He was waiting for the consolation of Israel which was divided into two as Northern Kingdom with inhabitants of ten tribes of Israel that was known as the "House of Israel" and the Southern Kingdom with the two tribes of Israel. Southern Kingdom was called the "House of Judah" from whose genealogy was David the king and from whose genealogy was Jesus Christ.

For many years from the time after King Solomon these two kingdoms were at war with each other. Jeroboam the king was the ruler of the "House of Israel" and Rehoboam the king was the ruler of the "House of Judah". Those who were in the "House of Judah" were only called as the "Jews". There have been successions of kings and there was no peace in Israel. At a time when Israel was under the Roman Government Jesus was born. It was a time when there was much disturbance in Israel and the inhabitants of both the kingdoms looked forward for peace.

It is at this time that an old man named Simeon who was just and devout and was looking forward to see consolation of Israel was comforted by the Holy Spirit. It was revealed to him by the Holy Spirit that he should not see death until he has seen Lord's Christ. Holy Spirit led him to the temple and he saw Jesus there. Joseph and Mary had brought Jesus there to the temple for the circumcision when eight days from his birth were accomplished. After the days of purification of Mary were completed in accordance with the Law of Moses Jesus was brought to the temple.

Leslie M. John

"Sanctify unto me all the firstborn, whatsoever openeth the womb among the children of Israel, both of man and of beast: it is mine". (Exodus 13:2)

Joseph and Mary offered a pair of turtle doves as sacrifice. Because they were considerably poor they could not offer a lamb as burnt offering but as an alternative as the provisions of Law permitted they offered turtle doves. (Cf. Leviticus 12:1-6)

Simeon saw the child Jesus and took him in his arms and blessed God and prayed that now that he saw the savior of the Gentiles he may allowed departing in peace. Simeon's testimony was great in that he said that he saw the salvation in Jesus and Jesus was the one whom the Father had prepared before the face of all the people and also that Jesus was the light to lighten the Gentiles, and the glory of His people Israel.

"A light to lighten the Gentiles, and the glory of thy people Israel" (Luke 2:32)

Joseph and Mary marveled when Simeon spoke those words. Simeon blessed them and said to them that Jesus was set for the fall of, and for the rising again of, many in Israel and for a sign which shall be spoken of. Simeon forewarned Mary that Jesus will suffer and his death shall put her to much grief. That was a forewarning for her to be prepared to see the death of Jesus in future.

Before the birth of Jesus Elizabeth, the mother of John the Baptist said:

"And whence is this to me, that the mother of my Lord should come to me?" (Luke 1:43)

"And Mary said, My soul doth magnify the Lord, And my spirit hath rejoiced in God my Saviour". (Luke 1:46-47)

Lord Jesus Christ was the Savior of Elizabeth and Mary. He is our Savior and salvation belongs to him. Whoever accepts Jesus as his/her Lord will be saved.

Leslie M. John

"Wherefore I give you to understand, that no man speaking by the Spirit of God calleth Jesus accursed: and that no man can say that Jesus is the Lord, but by the Holy Ghost". (1 Corinthians 12:3)

## SALVATION TO CORNELIUS

After Peter spoke to the congregation consisting people from various nations and tongues the message of salvation as we read in Acts Chapter 2, when the Holy Spirit fell on them and they all talked in many languages that could be understood by everyone, the gospel of Jesus Christ that peter gave to Cornelius, a Gentile, was a full message of grace, whereby a person can have salvation.

Peter spoke saying with God there is no partiality and that whoever works righteous and fears God is accepted by Him. Peter said that Jesus of Nazareth is the Lord of all, and that preached peace unto the children of Israel and the baptism that John preached. The word was published throughout Judea from Galilee. Jesus of Nazareth did miracles and healed the sick after he was anointed with the Holy Spirit and with power. Jesus also cast away evil spirits from those who were oppressed of the devil. Peter testified that The Father in heaven was with Jesus, the Son of God, and that the disciples were all witnesses to the preaching, and miracles of Jesus of Nazareth. They were witnesses to all that they saw in the land of Jews, and in Jerusalem, and yet Jesus was killed and he was hung on the Cross. God raised Jesus the third day and He appeared to all of them on different occasions and ate and drank with them. Peter said that Jesus asked them to preach to people that He was ordained of God to be the Judge of the quick and the dead. All the prophets spoke about Jesus and whoever believes in Him shall receive remission of sins. While Peter was still speaking Holy Spirit fell on all of them that heard the Gospel of Jesus Christ. The Jews, and the brethren, who came with Peter, were surprised to see that Holy Spirit fell on all of them to whom Gospel of Jesus Christ was preached. They all spoke in tongues and magnified God. Then Peter asked if there is any obstruction for them to be baptized in the name of the Lord and commanded them to be baptized in the name of the Lord. They requested Peter to stay with them for few more days. (Acts 10:19-48)

Leslie M. John

Apostles and brethren, who were in Judea, heard that Gentiles also received the word of God and they spoke in tongues. When Peter went to Jerusalem they argued with him as to why he went to Gentiles and ate with them. Their questioning was based on the instructions of Jesus who earlier said to them that they should not go in the way of Gentiles.

"These twelve Jesus sent forth, and commanded them, saying, Go not into the way of the Gentiles, and into any city of the Samaritans enter ye not" (Matthew 10:5)

Peter recollects this after Cornelius receives salvation that God was teaching him a lesson that whether it be Jew or Gentile, circumcised or un-circumcised, everyone who receives salvation is equal in the sight of God and none is 'common' or 'unclean'. Peter rehearsed before them the entire vision when he saw 'common' and 'unclean' animals in a vessel on a sheet that descended from heaven and a voice asked him to rise, kill and eat them; and that he refused. But the voice said to him that he should not call as 'common" and "unclean" that which God has cleansed (Acts 11:1-10).

## WAS CORNELIUS GRAFTED?

Cornelius became a member of "THE CHURCH".

Salvation to Gentiles was already in the plan of God. Israel is blinded in order that Gentiles may receive salvation. (Romans 11:6-8, 2 Corinthians 3:14)

Isaiah's prophecy was fulfilled by Jesus.

"That it might be fulfilled which was spoken by Esaias the prophet, saying, Behold my servant, whom I have chosen; my beloved, in whom my soul is well pleased: I will put my spirit upon him, and he shall shew judgment to the Gentiles. He shall not strive, nor cry; neither shall any man hear his voice in the streets. A bruised reed shall he not break, and smoking flax shall he not quench, till he send forth judgment unto victory. And in his name shall the Gentiles trust". (Matthew 12:17-21, Cf. Isaiah 42:3)

Leslie M. John

Abraham, who was the father of faith, was the root of Olive Tree. Gentiles, who are compared to wild Olive Tree, believed in Jesus as their savior, the unbelieving Jews were cut off and believing Gentiles were grafted into the Natural Olive Tree in their places and thereby Jews and Gentiles are made one in Christ. They became the body of Christ, and they are all collectively called the "bride" of Christ'. The Gentiles who believed Jesus as their savior were saved by grace through their faith in Jesus and became partakers of the root who is Abraham, who was known as father of faith. Both Abraham's descendants through Isaac, and Jacob, the believing Jews, along with unbelieving Gentiles are now the members the 'Church", whose head is Lord Jesus Christ, who identified himself as the true "vine".

"And if some of the branches be broken off, and thou, being a wild olive tree, wert graffed in among them, and with them partakest of the root and fatness of the olive tree" (Romans 11:17)

Apostle Paul's analogy of wild olive branches being grafted into natural olive tree is to mean that the Gentiles are made equal partners in the spiritual blessings along with Jews. Some of the natural branches were cut off because of their unbelief and in their place the wild olive branches are grafted. This is also not to mean that to accommodate Gentiles in the natural olive tree the branches of the natural branches were cut off, but because of their unbelief that the Jews, who are considered as natural olive branches, were cut off. The wild olive branches are asked not to take pride in themselves because they were grafted into natural olive tree. Paul warns that if natural branches were cut off because of their unbelief, God will not hesitate to cut off wild olive branches. This does not mean that salvation will be lost by any believer in Christ, but it only means that they will be cut off to make way for the natural branches.

Paul argues if God had cast away the natural branches and says "God forbid".

"I say then, Hath God cast away his people? God forbid. For I also am an Israelite, of the seed of Abraham, of the tribe of Benjamin" (Romans

Leslie M. John

11:1)".

 Here neither Peter nor Paul said that the Gentiles who believed in Jesus and were saved by grace through faith in Him became Jews first and then had the salvation, but the argument is that by faith in Jesus Christ Jews and Gentiles became one in Christ and Gentiles have become partakers of the faith of Abraham. There is no difference whether it is Jews or Gentiles, they are all one in Christ right from the period in Acts Chapter2 when three thousand were added to the Church, and Acts Chapter 10, where we see about salvation that was granted to an uncircumcised Gentile, Cornelius as also to others who were with him, and now and even until Jesus comes again to take his bride away.

"Then they that gladly received his word were baptized: and the same day there were added unto them about three thousand souls". (Acts 2:41)

 "While Peter yet spake these words, the Holy Ghost fell on all them which heard the word. And they of the circumcision which believed were astonished, as many as came with Peter, because that on the Gentiles also was poured out the gift of the Holy Ghost. For they heard them speak with tongues, and magnify God. Then answered Peter" (Acts 10:44-46)

The Church came into existence in Acts Chapter2 and the "One New Man" is the Church, which has members from Jewish community and from Gentiles. They are all one in Christ.

So we, being many, are one body in Christ, and every one members one of another. (Romans 12:5)

There is neither Jew nor Greek, there is neither bond nor free, there is neither male nor female: for ye are all one in Christ Jesus. (Galatians 3:28)

Leslie M. John

# CHAPTER 3
# GOD'S DEALING WITH ISRAEL

## ISRAEL

God named Jacob as Israel and loved Israel more than we can imagine. He has called Israel as His first born son.

It is not a name given by human but it is the name that is given by God; it is "Israel", which in Hebrew means God has striven, or God has saved. "And he said, Thy name shall be called no more Jacob, but Israel: for as a prince hast thou power with God and with men, and hast prevailed." Genesis 32:28. The descendants of Jacob are Israel. To be specific, the tribe of Judah, and the tribe of Benjamin, and those, who are from the tribe of Levi, who have joined with Judah are called, 'Jews'; and the rest of them are called, "Israel". God has given great privilege to the "Israel" as a whole to be called as His first born. "And thou shalt say unto Pharaoh, Thus saith the LORD, Israel is my son, even my firstborn" Exodus 4:22

A woman stricken with devil approached Jesus for healing of her daughter, crying "O Lord, thou Son of David; my daughter is grievously vexed with a devil" but Jesus replied, " ... I am not sent but unto the lost sheep of the house of Israel." Matthew 15:24. However, because of her faith in acknowledging her lowliness, when she said to Jesus, " yet the dogs eat of the crumbs which fall from their masters' table", "Then Jesus answered and said unto her, O woman, great is thy faith: be it unto thee even as thou wilt. And her daughter was made whole from that very hour". The woman was gentile; her plea was heard by Jesus because He had compassion on her. This is a mystery not seen in the Old Testament.

God blessed Abraham and said, whoever blesses Abraham will be blessed and whoever curses Abraham will be cursed, and likewise, God gave the privilege to Israel only to be called as Israel. Whoever calls himself/herself a 'Jew' or 'Israel', and not a Jew or Israel will face the

Leslie M. John

anger of the Lord. "I know thy works, and tribulation, and poverty, (but thou art rich) and I know the blasphemy of them which say they are Jews, and are not, but are the synagogue of Satan". Revelation 2:9.

It is very serious to identify oneself as "Jew" when one is not a Jew. Jacob and his descendants had all the priority in the presence of the Lord. "The portion of Jacob is not like them: for he is the former of all things; and Israel is the rod of his inheritance: The LORD of hosts is his name". Jeremiah 10:16

Yet, when it comes to the Church, the Church is His bride, heavenly possession. The Church stands over the Israel and the Jews. God fulfilled most of the covenants made to the children of Israel. The restoration of the kingdom unto them is yet to come. Jesus will reign from the throne of David for one thousand years after restoration of the kingdom to them. Unto this end the 'great tribulation' lasts and unto this end the delay occurs in the coming of Jesus again. Do not believe false prophets, false preachers, who predict the day of coming of Jesus. The Church will be 'caught up' when Jesus comes again.

For the Lord himself shall descend from heaven with a shout, with the voice of the archangel, and with the trump of God: and the dead in Christ shall rise first: Then we which are alive and remain shall be caught up together with them in the clouds, to meet the Lord in the air: and so shall we ever be with the Lord. (1 Thessalonians 4:16-17)

God is not finished with Israel yet. There is coming a time in future when they will face 'Great Tribulation' and will call upon the Lord to save them. It is then that God answers their prayers and make them One Kingdom. God will restore their Kingdom. God showed through this physical relationship of Hosea with Gomer, how Israel had turned away from God and become unfaithful to Him. Although God led them through wilderness, provided them food, clothing, shelter, protection, yet they worshipped idols.

The Northern Kingdom of Israel, which was called "the House of Israel" had built high places where they worshipped Baal, and Ashtaroth.

Leslie M. John

Southern Kingdom, which was called "the House of Judah" was no exception. They had also become unfaithful as we read in 2nd Chronicles 24:18

"And they left the house of the LORD God of their fathers, and served groves and idols: and wrath came upon Judah and Jerusalem for this their trespass". (2 Chronicles 24:18)

They are chastised severely for their unfaithfulness towards the Lord. Assyrians took captive of Northern Kingdom and Babylonians took captive of Southern Kingdom. The "House of Israel" which had ten tribes of Israel, was scattered. Many Jews of "House of Judah" returned to Jerusalem, but there are yet many more to return to Jerusalem. They all have gone astray and temporarily lost the love of God, who is still calling them and waiting for them to return to him.
It will not happen until the Church is taken away and they come under Antichrist, who will persecute them. It is then that they call upon the Lord to save them and God will answer their prayers. God chastised them several times and will yet chastise them, but He will never forsake them nor forget them, because they are His people and God made promises with their fathers, Abraham, Isaac, and Jacob, and He will keep up His promises. As hen gathers her children, God gathers them make them united and Jesus will reign over them as King.

God promised to that the children of Israel will be like the sand of the sea, which can not be measured or numbered. "...it shall come to pass, that in the place where it was said unto them, Ye are not my people, there it shall be said unto them, Ye are the sons of the living God. Then shall the children of Judah and the children of Israel be gathered together, and appoint themselves one head, and they shall come up out of the land: for great shall be the day of Jezreel. (Hosea 1:10-11)

God shows through the physical relationship the spiritual truth. Israel had become like prostitute to God, and yet He married them. In spite of Gomer bearing three children for Hosea, Gomer ran after money and luxury that she could not get from Hosea.

Leslie M. John

God says to Hosea to tell the children of his children through Gomer, to plead with their mother to return to their father and be united. God asks through prophets, and preachers to tell them to return to the Father. As long as they keep themselves away they will suffer.

Hosea spoke to "Lo-Ruhama" to tell her brethren, "Jezreel", and Lo-Ammi" to tell Gomer to return to Hosea. Here God calls them "Ammi" and "Ruhamah". Notice "Lo" is missing in their names. That is to show that God will keep up His promises to them even though they were unfaithful to Him, and will call them "My People". House of Israel and House of Judah will be united and they will have a peaceful life under their King Jesus Christ. (Hosea 2:1-5)

"God is a Spirit: and they that worship him must worship him in spirit and in truth". (John 4:24)

God is a Spirit and He cannot marry anyone, but He compares His relationship between Him and Israel to that of husband and wife. God applies physical relationship of Hosea with his wife Gomer to that of his own spiritual relationship with Israel and asks Israel to come back from her fallen stage to receive forgiveness.

God is compassionate and long-suffering and is waiting with his outstretched hands to receive them back into his fold. They have committed fornication and gone far from His love. They were unfaithful and worshipped idols. They worshipped Baal, a weather God, with the hope that it will give them good harvest that they become rich. They have worshipped Ashtaroth, a false god of Canaanites, said to be a god of fertility.

God hates idolatry and unfaithfulness. Israel was unfaithful to him. Similarly if born-again children are unfaithful to him, he will chastise. God will not allow his flock to be taken by anybody. Jesus is our Good Shepherd and he will not allow anyone to pluck his sheep from his fold.

The LORD God of Abraham, Jacob and Isaac is Jehovah, and He said...

"I am the LORD: that is my name: and my glory will I not give to another, neither my praise to graven images". (Isaiah 42:8)

The fore-runner of Jesus, John the Baptist preached saying"... Repent ye: for the kingdom of heaven is at hand". (Matthew 3:2) and Later Jesus preached "...Repent: for the kingdom of heaven is at hand". (Matthew 4:17). But then, notice how John introduced Jesus as:

"The next day John seeth Jesus coming unto him, and saith, Behold the Lamb of God, which taketh away the sin of the world" (John 1:29)

The phrases "kingdom of heaven", "kingdom of Christ", and "kingdom of God" are used interchangeably in the Gospels. Israel was in disturbed condition when Jesus came into this world. After King Solomon's death, the kingdom was divided into two and they never had peace. When Jesus was preaching "Repent: for the kingdom of heaven is at hand" the Jews understood that Jesus was preaching about the kingdom of Israel that was in disturbed condition. They expected their Messiah to come like a King and restore them their kingdom, but Jesus was born in a poor family of carpenter.

Jesus was from the lineage of David and he is called "Son of David". King Herod heard of Jesus and ordered the firstborn in the land of Judea to be killed because he was afraid of losing his own position. Shepherds were informed by the angels that a savior was born and he was Christ the savior. The wise men inquired of baby Jesus "Where is he that is born King of the Jews?" and went and worshipped him.

The prophecy of union of divided kingdom and the King is seen in Daniel's vision as we read in Daniel 7:13-14, 1 Kings 2:4, 8:25, Jeremiah 33:7. David's throne shall be established and there will be literal rein of Lord Jesus Christ from the throne of David.

"I saw in the night visions, and, behold, one like the Son of man came with the clouds of heaven, and came to the Ancient of days, and they brought him near before him. And there was given him dominion, and glory, and a kingdom, that all people, nations, and languages, should

Leslie M. John

serve him: his dominion is an everlasting dominion, which shall not pass away, and his kingdom that which shall not be destroyed". (Daniel 7:13-14)

After Jesus entered into ministry he said to his disciples not to go into the way of Gentiles but go to the lost sheep of the "house of Israel" and asked them to preach "The kingdom of heaven is at hand"

Jesus indeed came in search of the lost sheep of Israel:

"These twelve Jesus sent forth, and commanded them, saying, Go not into the way of the Gentiles, and into any city of the Samaritans enter ye not: But go rather to the lost sheep of the house of Israel. And as ye go, preach, saying, The kingdom of heaven is at hand." (Matthew 10:5-7)

 From the latter portions of Matthew it is clear that Jesus came not only for Jews but for all the mankind. He spoke his death, burial, and resurrection. After his resurrection and before his ascension he spoke of the Holy Spirit coming into the world after his ascension. Then, he gave commission to his disciples to preach first in Jerusalem, then in Judea and Samaria, and then to the uttermost part of the earth (Acts 1:8). That was the Gospel of Jesus Christ that Jesus asked his disciples to preach.

## THE TWO KINGDOMS

Previous knowledge of the division of Israel into two kingdoms, and their unfaithfulness toward God would be helpful to understand why God asked Prophet Hosea to marry Gomer, a woman, from the family of Prostitutes. Israel had become unfaithful to God and was divided into to two kingdoms. The northern kingdom was ruled by Jeroboam, and the southern kingdom was ruled by Rehoboam (1Kings 12:13, 14 and 1Kings 12:25-29).

The northern kingdom consisted of the ten tribes of Israelites, and the southern kingdom consisted of the tribe of Judah, and the tribe of Benjamin. The tribe of Levi, who were priests, got assimilated into both the regions. Later many from northern kingdom, who were loyal to king

Leslie M. John

David, migrated to the southern kingdom.

## THE HOUSE OF ISRAEL

It was the northern part of Israel that had the Ten Tribes of Jacob's sons, committed spiritual whoredom and was disloyal to God. They left their love toward living God, the God of Abraham, the God of Isaac, and the God of Jacob, and went after Baal, who was believed to be a god of fertility, who would grant her worshippers, sexual pleasures, and Ashtaroth, who was known as moon-god, and god of weather, who was believed to give her worshippers plenty of harvest.

These false hopes from these idols lured the entire northern kingdom, which was known as "House of Israel " and they worshiped them. Their prime intention was to have plenty of material possessions, wealth, and peace like those of other neighboring nation. They delighted in their worldly pleasures and have forgotten their first love.

The living God gave them all that they needed. He gave them food, clothing, shelter and protection right from the time they left Egypt where they were slaves and looked after them like His children, His possession, His nation, and His people. But then, Israel turned against God not once but several times.

 It is with this background that God asks Prophet Hosea to go and take unto himself a woman from the families of prostitutes and marry her. The word "Hosea " means "Joshua " or "Jesus " or "Salvation ". Hosea was a prophet in the northern kingdom of Israel, also called "House of Israel ". This was in the days of Jeroboam, king of Israel.

God spoke to Hosea and said to him to go and get a woman from among the prostitutes and marry her. Hosea goes and gets a woman named "Gomer " from among prostitutes and marries her. God was showing to Israelites their spiritual decline through these physical and visible signs.

The command from God came to Hosea to marry a woman from among prostitutes to show to the children of Israel that they have committed spiritual whoredom towards the Lord. They departed from their first love, just as the Church in Ephesus in the New Testament period, left her first love towards God. They departed from the living God and worshipped idols, which showed the unfaithfulness of Israelites, who were delivered by God from the bondage of slavery. They have become unfaithful like prostitutes to him.

Hosea's wife Gomer turned out to be unfaithful to Hosea and became a prostitute. In spite of God being faithful to them they have turned away from them and became worshippers of idols. God asked them not to worship idols and not to have any other gods before Him, but the children of Israel have set up idols in high places and worshipped Baal, and Ashtaroth.

"And they forsook the LORD, and served Baal and Ashtaroth ". (Judges 2:13)

## HOUSE OF JUDAH

The House of Judah was loyal to David and it consisted of the tribes of Judah and Benjamin. The House of Israel consisted of the Ten Tribes. The Levites, who were priests, got themselves assimilated into both the houses. Many others also migrated to the House of Judah and were loyal to the King David.

## HOSEA MARRIES GOMER

"The beginning of the word of the LORD by Hosea. And the LORD said to Hosea, Go, take unto thee a wife of whoredoms and children of whoredoms: for the land hath committed great whoredom, departing from the LORD " (Hosea 1:2)

## BAAL AND ASHTAROTH

The House of Israel built high places for Baal and Ashtoroth and worshipped them and mixed up with uncircumcised people in Judea and Samaria and lost their identity as true descendants of Israel. God sent His word through Prophet Hosea that He will scatter the 'House of Israel'

(Ten Tribes), and very soon Assyrians took captive of The Ten Tribes and the Ten Tribes got scattered.

As the time passed by the kings of the 'House of Judah' also did not fear the Lord. Babylonians took captive of the House of Judah. However, God in His mercy and as per the promise He made with Israel the "House of Israel" and the "House of Judah" will be together again. But this will happen only after they face Great Tribulation when they will call Messiah for their help. They will realize and acknowledge then that Jesus is the Messiah. They will have peace during the millennial rule by Lord Jesus Christ, who will rule literally for thousand years from the throne of David.

 In the New Testament we see Jesus who came into this world to seek the lost sheep of Israel had compassion on a Gentile woman who had faith in him. "But Jesus said unto her, Let the children first be filled: for it is not meet to take the children's bread, and to cast it unto the dogs. And she answered and said unto him, Yes, Lord: yet the dogs under the table eat of the children's crumbs" (Mark 7:27-28)

 In Acts Chapter 1 there is a description about the sequence to be followed as per the instructions of Lord Jesus Christ.(Acts 1:8). The Gospel was to be taken first to the Jew, next to Judea and Samaria, and then to the Gentiles.

Apostle Paul became the minister of Gospel to the Gentiles. Jesus is the way, the truth and the life. Man sinned and fell short of the glory of God. God Himself, in the form of man came into this world to die for us in order that we may have salvation if we believe in him. Jesus is the mediator between The Father and Man.

The Mosaic covenant, which was the shadow of the things to come, was not perfect in itself to secure salvation, but it was similar to a deposit that could be redeemed later.

Leslie M. John

# JEHU, JEZREEL, LO-RUHAMA, LO-AMMI

Jehu was the son of Nimshi, and he was the 10th king over Israel. When Elijah said that he was all alone left who did not bow to Baal, God said to him that he had reserved in Israel seven thousand, who did not bow unto Baal. God said that Jehu will slay all those escape from being killed by Hazael, who was king of Syria, and Elisha shall slay all those who escape being killed by Jehu, who was King over Israel (1 Kings 19:15-17).

Hazael, and Jehu were appointed to execute judgment of God and Jehu was given the responsibility of utterly destroying Ahab's house for promoting idolatry. Jezebel was thrown down from her window into the courtyard by Jehu's men, and she died. Later Jehu killed all the Baal-worshippers in Samaria (2 Kings 10:25-29). Jehu reigned in Samaria and not in Jezreel
However, "Jehu did not completely obey the commands of the Lord God of Israel. Instead, he kept doing the sinful things that Jeroboam had caused the Israelites to do" (2 Kings" (10:31) Jehu died and he was buried in Samaria. (2 Kings 10:35-36)

Jezreel was a city on the border of the territory of Issachar (Joshua 19:18) and by the wall of Jezreel Jezebel died and dogs ate her blood.

 "And of Jezebel also spake the LORD, saying, The dogs shall eat Jezebel by the wall of Jezreel" (1 Kings 21:23)

Although Jehu killed Jezebel and Baal-worshippers, he did not obey the command of the Lord fully and did for his personal gain. He allowed sinful things that Jeroboam had caused the Israelites to do. That is the reason why God said to Hosea to call his first born as "Jezreel".
Gomer conceived by Hosea and gave birth to a son, whose name was given by God as "Jezreel". "Jezreel" is a Hebrew word, which figuratively means "sow" or "dissiminate" God named the firstborn of Hosea as "Jezreel" to show that He would scatter the Ten tribes of the northern kingdom also called the "House of Israel" as a result of their sin against the Lord.

Leslie M. John

God said that He would avenge the blood of Jezreel upon the house of Jehu and will cause to end the "House of Israel" that is he would scatter the ten tribes of northern kingdom of Israel.

Later Gomer conceives by Hosea and gives birth to a daughter, whom God named as "Lo-ruhamah" which is to mean that God will not have mercy upon the "House of Israel" but will scatter them away for their unfaithfulness toward Him. At the same God says that he will have mercy on the "House of Judah", which was the southern kingdom of Israel.

As soon as "Lo-ruhamah" was weaned Gomer bore another son by Hosea and God called the child "Lo-Ammi", which means that they are not God's people and He would not be their God. Yet, God says the number of the children of Israel shall be as the sand of the sea that cannot be numbered and it shall come to pass where it was said that the children of Israel were not God's people, they will, then be called the sons of the living God.

The children of Judah and the children of Israel shall be gathered together and God calls them "Ammi" which was to mean that they are his people and "Ruhama" which was to mean that God will have mercy on them.

Leslie M. John

# CHAPTER 4
# PREDESTINAITON

"Predestination" is a very vigorously debated topic for many years now. The exposition that I present here is as I understand and as revealed to me by the Holy Spirit.

"Predestination" is a biblical doctrine and if it is understood correctly our hope in Lord Jesus Christ and in our eternity increases, thus honoring God for loving us.

It should be understood that "Predestination" emphasizes on the end result than that of intermediate stages.

Predestination is a doctrine of God marking out the believers in Christ to conform to the image of His Son. But then, we cannot skip meditating on Salvation because only those who are saved will be conformed to the image of His Son. Our gratitude towards God increases when we understand that God did not predestinate some to destruction and some to salvation but He predestinated sons adopted by Him to be conformed to the image of His Son, Lord Jesus Christ.

It is a wrong notion that God prepared vessels of wrath before the foundation of the world in order to glorify the vessels of mercy. If we take into consideration the statistics of ever growing population in the world that includes God's chosen people, the Israel, and the deaths that have occurred from first century onwards it is unbelievable that many still say God predestinated so many billions of people for destruction. God's love towards man is exceedingly great and His offering of His only begotten Son as sacrifice for the remission of our sins is grossly misinterpreted by some to add the advantage only to those limited ones, who, they believe, would respond to the call of God irresistibly. Bible asserts that God is love and it is He who loved us first, not that we loved Him first. God predestinated us in his foreknowledge and called us to believe in Him, but the onus of believing on Lord Jesus Christ as one's personal savior is on man.

Leslie M. John

"Jesus saith unto him, I am the way, the truth, and the life: no man cometh unto the Father, but by me". (John 14:6)

"For God so loved the world, that he gave his only begotten Son, that whosoever believeth in him should not perish, but have everlasting life" John 3:16

While it is true that no one comes to the Father except through Lord Jesus Christ it is also true that only those who believe in Lord Jesus Christ shall not perish, but have everlasting life. The responsibility of believing in Lord Jesus Christ rests on man. God does not force anyone to believe in Him nor does man respond irresistibly to God's call. At the same time man's will is not greater than God's will and man cannot by himself do anything against the will of God.

Apostle Paul wrote those words in Romans 8:29-30 and Ephesians 1:5, 11 for the edification of believers in Christ; not in any way to cause divisions among Christians. The Scriptures give us great hope of being confirmed to the Son of God, Lord Jesus Christ, but this is yet future. The prophecies are written in past tense and many of them are fulfilled and many of them are yet to be fulfilled. The hope given to the believers in Christ that they will be confirmed to the image of His Son is yet to be fulfilled.

It is interesting to note that Satan takes out the same phrases that God intended as hope for the believers and uses them to cause divisions among them. Satan side tracks the issue at hand and puts believers into debate as to whether God predestinated some to salvation and some to destruction. Consequently one section of the believers keeps arguing that God predestined some to salvation and the rest to destruction. There is another section of believers, who argue that God predestinated some to salvation and we should not say God predestined others for destruction. The debate continues and man struggles to evolve a solution ultimately bringing dishonor to God and honor to Satan. That is what Satan intends to do.

Leslie M. John

# TO BE CONFORMED TO THE IMAGE OF CHRIST

While dealing with this subject of predestination it becomes necessary to expound few verses.

"For whom he did foreknow, he also did predestinate to be conformed to the image of his Son, that he might be the firstborn among many brethren. Moreover whom he did predestinate, them he also called: and whom he called, them he also justified: and whom he justified, them he also glorified". (Romans 8:29-30)

God said as many as are led by the Spirit of God, they are the sons of God and the sons of God have not received the spirit of bondage again to fear but received the spirit of adoption. This privilege entails us to call God as "Abba, Father" and the Spirit bears witness that we are the children of God. (Romans 8:14-16)

Apostle Paul explains that the heir as long as he is a child does not differ from a servant because even though he is the lord of all, he is under tutor and governors until the time appointed of the father. The children are still considered as in bondage under the elements of the world. But when the fullness of time was come God sent His one only begotten Son, born of the virgin Mary, conceived of the Holy Ghost, made under law, to redeem that was under the law that we might receive the adoption of sons. Therefore, we are no more servants but sons and daughters, and if it is so, then we are heirs of God through Christ.

Lord Jesus Christ redeemed us from the bondage of Mosaic Law and gave us the liberty to be under the provisions of Gospel to gain the privilege of being the adopted sons and receive the full benefits promised to the children of Israel. Even though the promises, covenants and law belonged to the children of Israel, yet, now those who accept Lord Jesus Christ as savior are set free from the stringent Laws of Moses. Our salvation is by grace through faith. (Galatians 4:1-7).

It was according to God's good pleasure of His will that Gentiles are also made equal partners of the inheritance of heavenly blessings. Now, therefore, in this dispensation there is no difference between Jew and

Leslie M. John

Gentile. A Jew has to come to the Lord Jesus Christ just as any Gentile would come and accept Him as the Savior. Jesus is the only way, the Truth, and the Life and no one can come to the Father except through Him.

If Jews need heavenly blessings and are desirous of being conformed, in future, to the image of Lord Jesus Christ, who relinquished His glory when He came into this world as a servant in the form of man, was crucified, died, buried and rose from the dead with uncorrupted body, in his glorified body, ascended into heaven, and seated on the right hand of the Majesty, then they necessarily have to accept Lord Jesus Christ as their Messiah. If they continue to be in rebellion of the Gospel of Jesus Christ, then, according to the word of God, they lose that privilege of being conformed to the image of His Son in eternity.

"Having predestinated us unto the adoption of children by Jesus Christ to himself, according to the good pleasure of his will" (Ephesians 1:5)

"In whom also we have obtained an inheritance, being predestinated according to the purpose of him who worketh all things after the counsel of his own will" (Ephesians 1:11)

God predestines us unto the adoption as children by Lord Jesus Christ to Himself according to the good pleasure of His will. In Him we have obtained an inheritance according to the purpose of Him. The very first assertion the scripture makes here is that God foreknew those who would be conformed to the image of his Son, Lord Jesus Christ. Therefore, God predestined those who, in his foreknowledge, would respond to His call and accept Lord Jesus Christ as their savior. Those, who respond and confess their sins to Lord Jesus Christ, will be forgiven of their sins and justified. They are assured of being confirmed, in future, to the image of his son and, therefore, He called them and will glorify them in eternity.

Surely God foreknew those who would be conformed to the image of his Son. Therefore, he called them and justified and glorified them. None of these assertions add emphasis to imaginations that God predestined some to hell or God forcibly converts any human to his side. The Bible

Leslie M. John

contains message of Gospel of Jesus Christ and the message is that Lord Jesus Christ is the Savior, that He is the Son of God, that He and the Father are one, and that there is no salvation outside of Him. Jesus is the way, the truth and the light.

"And not only they, but ourselves also, which have the firstfruits of the Spirit, even we ourselves groan within ourselves, waiting for the adoption, to wit, the redemption of our body" (Romans 8:23)

"Who are Israelites; to whom pertaineth the adoption, and the glory, and the covenants, and the giving of the law, and the service of God, and the promises" (Romans 9:4)
"To redeem them that were under the law, that we might receive the adoption of sons" (Galatians 4:5)

It was God's good pleasure that according to His will he predestined us unto adoption of children by Jesus Christ. Man has no free will to do anything against the will of God to be predestined either to become the child of God or to go against God. It is God who controls men's will. Man can by himself do nothing other than choosing for himself eternal damnation by rejecting Jesus as Savior. There is difference between choice a man makes and the will that he has. Men's will is not free to make any decision against God's will but men can make their choices. The Will of men cannot overpower God's will.

The will of God is all powerful and God makes the world to move according to His will, and yet he provides a choice and chance for man to repent of his sin and choose the living God. Jehovah is living God and not an idol. Idols do not move, do not speak, and do not do anything on their own. Jehovah is the living God who loved us and gave His one and only begotten Son to be crucified for our sake in order that we might be saved from perishing. Whosoever believes in Jesus as Savior will not perish but will have everlasting life.

There is inheritance promised to those who believe in Lord Jesus Christ as Savior and we are predestinated to have that inheritance in future and to be conformed to the image of His Son. This is according to the purpose of Him who works all things according to the counsel of His own

Leslie M. John

will. Jehovah does not need our counsel and His counsel and His purposes are final. The image of God is lost in the Garden of Eden when man committed transgression against the will of God and sinned against God's law. God is the creator and man is under His will and His purposes, yet man has the choice to choose the better or worse.

The first man exercised his choice in a bad way and lost the image of God. In His mercy God desires to restore that lost image to all those who have sinned. Bible says there is no one righteous; not even one and everyone has come short of the glory of God. If we say that we have not sinned, then we make God a liar. The only way to get out of that bad situation and to be conformed to the image of the Son, Lord Jesus Christ, is to repent of sins and turn to God and accept that Lord Jesus Christ is the only Savior.

Careful reading of Romans Chapter 9 reveals God's dealing with the children of Israel. Apostle Paul was a Jew and belonged to the tribe of Benjamin (Philippians 3:5). He expresses his concern for the children of Israel. The first five verses speak of his continual sorrow in his heart for them because they rejected Jesus Christ as their Messiah. He wishes that he could be accursed if his brethren and kinsmen, to whom belonged the adoption, the glory and the covenants and the giving of the Law, accepted Jesus Christ as their Savior.

In discussions about Predestination and Freewill often there is a tendency to say first of all, predestination is all about salvation while it is all about conforming to the image of Lord Jesus Christ and secondly compare —

1. The choosing of Jacob by God over Esau
2. Power over vessels of wrath and over vessels of Mercy
3. Pharaoh's heart that was hardened.

Apostle Paul narrates about God's choice of Jacob over Esau and how they struggled with each other even when they were in the womb of Rebecca. God chose Jacob over Esau and blessed him. Jacob became father of the twelve tribes. God renamed Jacob as "Israel" and called the children of Israel as "My People".

Leslie M. John

Therefore my people shall know my name: therefore they shall know in that day that I am he that doth speak: behold, it is I. (Isaiah 52:6)

Can anyone question God's actions? No. God said that He will have mercy and compassion on who He decides to have compassion.

For he saith to Moses, I will have mercy on whom I will have mercy, and I will have compassion on whom I will have compassion. (Romans 9:15)

This verse is grossly misinterpreted that God has arbitrarily chose Jacob over Esau and rendered Esau and all others as vessels of wrath. God choose Jacob in His mercy and blessed Him but that does not mean He has decided to treat all others in His wrath or predestinated them for Hell. Can a vessel say to the potter as to why the potter made it vessel unto honor and the other for dishonor?

"Hath not the potter power over the clay, of the same lump to make one vessel unto honour, and another unto dishonour?" (Romans 9:21)

Vessels of wrath were not marked out or selected before the foundation of the world, but the vessels of mercy were marked out before the foundation to be conformed to the image of Lord Jesus Christ. Everyone has the opportunity to come to the Lord and accept Him as the Savior and have everlasting life. God has the power to make His own decision whom to choose for bestowing His blessings upon them. As Paul writes who can find fault with God and who can resist His will?

God raised Pharaoh that His glory may be manifest but at the same time God cannot be held guilty of Pharaoh's hardening of heart. Close look at few verses reveal that God hardened Pharaoh's heart after Pharaoh hardened his heart. God made firm the hardening of heart by Pharaoh because Pharaoh, as evil as he was, harassed the children of Israel and hardened his heart against them. In Romans Chapter 1 also similar theme is seen.

When man hardens his heart and chooses to be in sin God allows him to

Leslie M. John

harden his heart more and hands him over to his sin. Every sin has consequences and man is responsible for the consequences that follow after committing sin. Many diseases in man are the result of sin and the consequences of sin become like stench in the nostrils of man ever trying to get rid of them.

Example is seen in one of the plagues that was removed by God as Moses prayed to the Lord based on Pharaoh's request frogs died but the heaps of frogs were still left behind for Pharaoh's people to gather them and the land stank. This is how sin leaves behind in a man something that reminds it. However, we should be glad the Lord does not remember our sins that are pardoned. (Exodus 8:13-14, Hebrews 10:17)

The phrase "I will harden his heart" used by God occurs in Exodus 4:21, Exodus 7:3, Exodus 14:4, Exodus 14:17 but then these verses show us that God hardened Pharaoh's heart only after Pharaoh chose to harden his heart. That is to say God made sure that the hardening of heart of Pharaoh was firm after his own desire and actions. (Cf. Exodus 8:15, 19, 32, 34; 9:34)

"Wherefore then do ye harden your hearts, as the Egyptians and Pharaoh hardened their hearts? when he had wrought wonderfully among them, did they not let the people go, and they departed?" (1 Samuel 6:6)

God provided the circumstances and the occasion for Pharaoh to make a decision and Pharaoh made decision to harden his heart and God approved his decision. Pharaoh is guilty of his decision. Similarly, Pilate is guilty of his choice of handing over Jesus Christ to be crucified.

The LORD commanded Moses to say to the children of Israel to choose either blessing by following the LORD or to choose the curse by not following the LORD. As we see later Israel stumbled many times and was chastised severely.

"I call heaven and earth to record this day against you, that I have set before you life and death, blessing and cursing: therefore choose life, that both thou and thy seed may live" (Deuteronomy 30:19)

Leslie M. John

Prophet Hosea spoke the word of the LORD and said about the children of Israel that they were like prostitute cheating upon her husband. Paul picks up what Hosea spoke about them from Hosea Chapters 1-3 and quotes them in Romans 9:25 that the children of Israel were called as "Lo-ruhama" and "Lo-Ammi" which mean that the LORD will have no mercy upon the house of Israel and will utterly take them away (Hosea 1:6) and that they are not His people and He will not be their God (Hosea 1:9). But God does not leave them in such condition but will have mercy upon them when they repent of their sin and turn to the LORD as we read in Hosea 1:10 and Hosea 2:1

"Yet the number of the children of Israel shall be as the sand of the sea, which cannot be measured nor numbered; and it shall come to pass, that in the place where it was said unto them, Ye are not my people, there it shall be said unto them, Ye are the sons of the living God". (Hosea 1:10)

"Say ye unto your brethren, Ammi; and to your sisters, Ruhamah" (Hosea 2:1).

A passage from Jeremiah 18:6-12 also shows us that man has choice to choose what he wants to choose and face the consequences and that God does not force upon him God's choices. God reveals to man His glory and the way to obtain salvation but the onus of accepting God's revelation and choosing of glory and salvation is on the man. If only God forces upon man the salvation without giving any opportunity for man to decide for himself the salvation, the blessings, the conforming to the image of His Son, the very purpose of giving his disciples commission to preach the Gospel of Jesus Christ was of no purpose.

Surely God is sovereign and man has no free will because man cannot do anything against God by his own will and yet wicked is left to exercise his choice to choose either salvation or destruction. The wicked will be in hell by their own choice and it is not according to the purposes of God nor were they created or set apart to be so before the foundation of the world was laid by God. God in his foreknowledge marked out those who would believe in Him to be conformed to the image of His Son and they

Leslie M. John

are the ones who respond to the call of the Gospel of Jesus Christ.

The believers in Christ are chosen to be conformed to the image of Christ and that is yet to be fulfilled. The believers are given the status of adopted sons and as Apostle Paul writes in Galatians Chapter 4. The heir is a child and does have more status than that of a servant though he is lord of all because he is still under tutors and governors until the time appointed by the father. Similarly when the fullness of time was come God sent His only begotten Son, who was born of the virgin, made under law and we, who were under the bondage of sin, are redeemed from the Mosaic Law that we might receive the adoption of sons.

Now, because we the believers in Christ are the sons, God gave us the privilege to call the Father as "Abba, Father". Therefore, we have no more a status of a servant, but of a son, and because we have that status as son, we heirs of God through Christ (Galatians 4:1-7). Our bodies are made of dust and these bodies must return to dust. Until then we sweat and eat food that we have through our toil, and return to dust in the fullness of the time that God has appointed (Genesis 3:19).

After we return to dust our spirit goes to be with the Lord. As the Scriptures say we must all appear before the judgment seat of Christ that we may receive the rewards, whether they are good or bad, that we have done in our bodies (2 Corinthians 5:6-11). As we are in this world with the physical bodies that God has given us our bodies are subject to the consequences of our sin until these bodies are redeemed when the Lord comes again. The Lord himself descends from heaven with the voice of the archangel, and with the trump of God.

The dead will rise first and those who are alive then will be caught up together with them in the clouds to the meet the Lord in the air and be with the Lord for ever and ever. (1 Thessalonians 4:16-17). Man is sinner by birth through Adam but will be made alive as the Scripture says: "For as in Adam all die, even so in Christ shall all be made alive". (1 Corinthians 15:22). It is a mystery revealed to us that we will not all die but shall be changed in a moment in the twinkling of an eye at the last trump when the trumpet sounds, and the dead are raised incorruptible.

Leslie M. John

God gives us bodies according to His pleasure. 1 Corinthians 15:38, 51-52)

In Romans Chapter 8 to 11 Paul brings out sublime thoughts on how God gave the opportunity for Gentiles to come to His presence by blinding the understanding of Jews until the fullness of time of Gentiles be come in. The Jews in this dispensation of "Church", the body of Christ, whose head is the Lord Jesus Christ, should come to him just as Gentiles. There is no difference between Jews and Gentiles in this dispensation.

Those Jews who are defying God's commandments of accepting Jesus Christ as Messiah are missing heavenly blessings promised for believers in Christ in Ephesians Chapter 1. God chose a nation for himself and gave them His name and called them as "My People" Old Testament prophets prophesied about the coming of the Messiah, and when Lord Jesus Christ, the Messiah came as prophesied they rejected Him. They expect their Messiah would come like a king but Jesus came into this world in the form of a servant in the likeness of man to redeem them and also all of us from the bondage of sin by offering Himself as the sacrifice on the cross of Calvary.

There is no necessity to offer animals as sacrifice any more as those sacrifices only covered sins, but could not remit the sins fully. The blood of Jesus Christ shed for everyone is always available to cleanse from sins of anyone who accepts Him as the Messiah. Confession of sins and accepting Lord Jesus Christ as one's Savior makes one the child of God and to have everlasting life. The saved child of God will be with the Lord for ever  having been conformed to the image of Christ that which is promised in the doctrine of Predestination presented in Romans Chapter 8:28-29 and in Ephesians Chapter 1. But then, those Jews, who have rejected Him as Savior and those in future, who would be left-behind, after the Church (the body of Christ, also known as the "Bride of Christ" will be judged at the "Sheep and Goat Judgment" detailed in Matthew Chapter 25. God deals with them in His own way and we are not authorized to judge their destiny. All that we are commanded to do is to "Pray for the peace of Jerusalem"

Leslie M. John

"Pray for the peace of Jerusalem: they shall prosper that love thee".
(Psalms 122:6)

Lord Jesus Christ how the kingdom of heaven will be as we read in
Matthew 20:1-16. It is like a man, a house holder, who went out early in
the morning to hire laborers to work in his vineyard. He went in search of
them early in the morning and hired laborers with an agreement that he
would pay a penny a day.

The laborers agreed and went into work in his vineyard. The man went
about the third hour and saw some other standing idle in the market
place and said to them to go and work in his vineyard promising them
their wages as are right in his sight. They went into work in his vineyard.
Likewise, he hired some more at sixth hour, ninth hour and eleventh
hour. Those who came into his vineyard were idling without work, but
the man gave work to them in his compassion.

At the end of the day the man said to his steward to call all the laborers
starting from those who were hired early in the morning to those who
were hired at the eleventh hour. Remember the man entered into
agreement to those who were hired early in the morning that he would
pay them a penny a day and they agreed. When it was time to distribute
the wages the man paid to the laborers who came in to work at eleventh
hour at the rate of a penny a day. Then, those who came in to work early
in the morning thought they would receive more than a penny a day as
any man's logic in this would say.

But then, God gave every one equal wages according to His riches in his
mercy without breaching upon the agreement made with those who
came in to work early in the morning. Those who came first into work in
the vineyard murmured against the man who treated everyone alike. But
the man said to them that he did no wrong to them because lawfully he
gave out of his abundance as he chose without breaking the agreement
made with them. Similar would be the Kingdom of God, where the first
would be made last and the last first as God decides.

We are no judges to judge the actions of God and His mercy (Matthew

Leslie M. John

20:1-16). There are instances where we see God punished those who ill-treated Jews even though God called the children of Israel as "stiff necked". It is God who called them "stiff necked" but no man can take the advantage of God's calling them as "stiff necked" and call them so.

"For he saith to Moses, I will have mercy on whom I will have mercy, and I will have compassion on whom I will have compassion". (Romans 9:15)

Salvation belongs to the Lord Jesus Christ and He said "...I am the way, the truth, and the life: no man cometh unto the Father, but by me". (John 14:6)

Obviously, there is no way other than Lord Jesus Christ to have everlasting life and no man can go the Father except through Him. No one can earn salvation through his good works or good behavior but the only way to everlasting life is to believe in the sacrificial death of Lord Jesus Christ for our sins and confess our sins to him. If you confess with your mouth the Lord Jesus Christ and believe in your heart that God raised him from the dead you will be saved.

 "That if thou shalt confess with thy mouth the Lord Jesus, and shalt believe in thine heart that God hath raised him from the dead, thou shalt be saved" (Romans 10:9)

It is the only way to conformed to the image of Lord Jesus Christ in eternity. No one would want the image of fallen Adam, who, before the fall had all the glory in creation and was given dominion over the fish of the sea, over the fowl of the air, and over every living thing that moves on the earth although he was made of dust. In his fall he lost many blessings and the earth was cursed for him. He was asked to toil hard and in his sweat he would earn food for him.

"And God blessed them, and God said unto them, Be fruitful, and multiply, and replenish the earth, and subdue it: and have dominion over the fish of the sea, and over the fowl of the air, and over every living thing that moveth upon the earth". (Genesis 1:28)

Leslie M. John

Whenever man is in comfortable and blessed state he tends to turn against the will of God. The children of Israel were given "manna" from heaven and protection from God when they were journeying in the wilderness but they murmured all the time. God commanded them not to worship any other idol but they made calf of gold and worshipped it. Even after reaching Canaan, and many years later they worshipped Baal, and Ashtaroth in high places and angered Jehovah. The children of Israel rebelled against the Jehovah not once or twice but several times until they were plucked out from the land of Israel and scattered throughout the world. God is waiting for them eagerly to return to Him but they chose to reject Jesus Christ as the Messiah.

Prophets spoke about Lord Jesus Christ, but when He was on this earth, they cried out before the Pilate that His blood may be upon them yet crucify Him. Rightly so, as they desired, Titus went and destroyed the whole land of Israel not leaving one stone upon the other of their blessed Temple Jerusalem, in AD 70. The children of Israel were killed and harassed beyond anyone could imagine. They still choose to be under the Old Testament laws and yet not fully obeying all the Ten Commandments.

It was known fact that no one could keep all the Ten Commandments, neither was it possible to sacrifice animals for the covering of their sins year after year, yet they choose to follow what is in the Old Testament and fail on many counts. Jesus came to fulfill the law and removed the yoke of circumcision, yoke of Mosaic Law, and ended the necessity of animal sacrifices, yet they choose to live under the yoke and fail to fulfill all that was required of them by God. Lord Jesus became propitiation for not only them but for all and died as substitution for all mankind.

Whoever confesses his sins to Lord Jesus Christ He will not only forgive their sins, but justify the one who confesses his sing to him, as pure, righteous, and holy. It is so unfortunate that the children of Israel, whom God loved so much and called them as "My People" still, stand in rebellion against God and do not accept Jesus Christ as their Messiah.

If only they accept Jesus as their savior and as the Son of God and

Leslie M. John

believe in Him, God was willing to conform them to the image of Lord Jesus Christ, but they choose to live under the yoke of Old Testament laws and have earthly blessings rather than heavenly blessings promised to the "body of Christ". Hebrews 10:26 says that if we sin willfully after receiving the knowledge of the truth there is more sacrifices left for neither Jew nor Gentile for the remission of sins. It is only the belief in the sacrificial death of Lord Jesus Christ that can save a man from perishing.

"For if we sin wilfully after that we have received the knowledge of the truth, there remaineth no more sacrifice for sins" (Hebrews 10:26)

Lord Jesus Christ became propitiation and substitution and promised to justify anyone who comes to Him and accept Him as Lord and Savior, but then Jews still remain in rebellion to the invitation He gave them. Lord Jesus Christ died upon the cross of Calvary bearing sins of every one and yet the Jews desire to be under Old Covenant. It is proved beyond doubt that it is impossible to keep all the Ten Commandments given by the God through Moses, yet, they prefer to remain under them. When the Church, the body of Christ, the bride of Christ is caught up on Jesus coming again, they would be left behind still in rebellion to the invitation of accepting Him as the Messiah.

After the resurrection and ascension of Lord Jesus Christ the Gospel message was being proclaimed by His disciples when there came down from Judea and taught the brethren that they should be circumcised as Mosaic Law prescribed otherwise, they said, there would not be salvation. This was nothing but laying heavy yoke on those who are freed by Lord Jesus Christ. The salvation is purely by the grace of God through faith in Him and accepting Lord Jesus Christ as Savior and by confessing sins to Him that He may forgive them. But the Pharisees and Scribes lay heavy burden on the people that Mosaic Law should still be observed to receive salvation.

When Paul and Barnabas came to know about such insistence, there arose no small dissensions and disputation with them. In the council at Jerusalem it was resolved even with Peter endorsing the teaching of Paul

Leslie M. John

is according the desire of Lord Jesus Christ (Acts 15:1-5)

The realization that Lord Jesus Christ is the Messiah and the stringent Mosaic Law is outdated comes in them only when they are subject to the "Great Tribulation" under Antichrist, and every knee will bow then to Lord Jesus Christ and accept Him as the Messiah.

Leslie M. John

# CHAPTER 5
# WORSHIP

**G**od wants us to worship him in spirit and truth. The whole purpose of God sending His only begotten Son was to reconcile man unto himself and grant him everlasting life. There is no difference between Jew and Gentile in Christ.

"Forasmuch as ye know that ye were not redeemed with corruptible things, as silver and gold, from your vain conversation received by tradition from your fathers" (1 Peter 1:18)

"Behold, the days come, saith the LORD, that I will make a new covenant with the house of Israel, and with the house of Judah: Not according to the covenant that I made with their fathers in the day that I took them by the hand to bring them out of the land of Egypt; which my covenant they brake, although I was an husband unto them, saith the LORD" (Jeremiah 31:31-32)

Inside of this bigger picture of reconciling man to himself comes the Davidic Covenant and God's promise of restoring the kingdom of Israel. The "House of Israel" and the "House of Judah" will be united and Jesus will reign as king over them. In spite of the children of Israel committing sin and were unfaithful to God, He will love them, and promised them that He will have mercy upon them because they are His people and they shall say "Thou art my God" (Hosea 2:23).

God is angry over them because they broke his covenant even though he took them by hand to bring them out of the land of Egypt and considered himself as an husband to them. He is asking them to come back to him.

"Turn, O backsliding children, saith the LORD; for I am married unto you: and I will take you one of a city, and two of a family, and I will bring you to Zion": (Jeremiah 3:14)

Leslie M. John

If they do not repent and still stand as obstinate as they stood while Jesus was on this earth, God will make them to fall on their knees and cry for help. God will surely answer their prayers and unite the "House of Israel" and the "House of Judah". That will be the fulfillment of the new covenant in respect of the children of Israel.

Apostle Paul referred to the relationship of God and Israel in Romans 9:25-26 ("Osee" is a form of writing of the word Hosea in Hebrew)

"As he saith also in Osee, I will call them my people, which were not my people; and her beloved, which was not beloved. And it shall come to pass, that in the place where it was said unto them, Ye are not my people; there shall they be called the children of the living God". (Romans 9:25-26)

But is that all the Bible about? No, God was dealing with them to show to you and me the way we were unfaithful but when we confessed our sins to him he has washed our sins away. Restoring the kingdom was not the only purpose that Jesus came into this world. No doubt, he came seeking the lost sheep of Israel, but he came to die for you and me. Jesus asked us to remember his death for our sake.

Lord Jesus Christ rose form the dead on the third day and after forty days he ascended into heaven. He will come back soon. Jesus came into this world to save you and me. Jesus asked us to remember his death for our sake. He rose from the dead on the third day and after forty days he ascended into heaven. He will come back soon.

Don't be misguided that the "New Covenant" is for Jews only...Some Christians misinterpret that it is not as we read in Matthew 26:28 Mark 14:24 Luke 22:20 1Corinthians 11:25

## LORD'S SUPPER

And as they were eating, Jesus took bread, and blessed it, and brake it, and gave it to the disciples, and said, Take, eat; this is my body. And he took the cup, and gave thanks, and gave it to them, saying, Drink ye all of it; For this is my blood of the new testament, which is shed for many for the remission of sins". (Matthew 26:26-28)

Page 70

Leslie M. John

There are four clear references (Matthew 26:26, Mark 14:22, Luke 22:19 and 1 Corinthians 11:24) where Lord Jesus Christ said, 'take eat; this is my body'. Likewise there are four clear references where Lord Jesus Christ said, 'my blood'.

Matthew, Mark and John, and Apostle Paul wrote that when Lord Jesus broke the bread he said 'take, eat; this is my body'. Luke, the historian, who touched the different themes of the subject did not write chronologically but included some other facts for us to ponder on. Likewise, after breaking the bread, the Lord took cup and when he had supped said, 'This cup is the new testament in my blood; this do ye, as oft as ye drink, in remembrance of me.

Each word said by Lord Jesus Christ at the time of Lord's Supper carries great significance. From Matthew 26:26 the noticeable phrases are: "As they were eating", "Jesus took bread", "and blessed it", "and brake it", "and gave it" , "to the disciples, "and said", "Take eat"; "this is my body"

"As they were eating" (Matt. 26:26) or "And as they did eat" (Mark 14:22) signifies that the Lord's Supper was instituted by Lord Jesus Christ, immediately after the Passover feast celebration.

The context where Jesus said, 'this is my body" in Gospels, appears at a place where there is description about Passover celebration. It was on the first day of the feast of unleavened bread; obviously it was on the night before his crucifixion. This has direct reference to the lamb that was killed one day before the 14th Nissan by the children of Israel in the land of Egypt in obedience to the commandment of LORD through Moses and Aaron to escape from the tenth plague that was brought by the LORD in Egypt.

The firstborn of every Egyptian, including that of Pharaoh, was killed on the night when the LORD Passed over the land. The LORD redeemed the children of Israel, who were in bondage of slavery under Pharaoh. Every firstborn of the children of Israel and their household was spared from the wrath of the LORD, because they did as He commanded them to do. They were asked to kill the lamb, set apart for this purpose, on the fourteenth day of the first month of the first year and strike its blood on

Leslie M. John

the lintels and door posts of their houses.

The LORD did as He said to them and passed over their homes on seeing the blood of the lamb on the lintels and door posts of their homes. The next morning they left the Egypt and enjoyed freedom.

The children of Israel were asked to keep Passover forever. Jesus, who came not to break the law, but to fulfill it, kept the Passover just before his crucifixion exactly as was required of him to do and in compliance to the instructions that were given in Exodus Chapter 12. It was the Passover feast day, and the disciples of Jesus asked him as to where would he have the feast of unleavened bread.

Luke's account of the Passover feast and Lord's Supper give few extra details such as a Jesus telling his disciples to follow a man bearing a pitcher of water, an unusual scene among Jews. The disciples are asked to follow him into the house where he enters.

The disciples then were supposed to ask the man of the house that the Master wants to know where the guest chamber is, where He along with the disciples would eat the Passover meal. The man of the house shows a large upper room where Jesus would eat the Passover meal. The disciples did just as the Master, Lord Jesus told them to do.

Leslie M. John

# CHAPTER 6
# THE OLD COVENANT AND
# THE NEW COVENANT

God cherished relationship with man and He desired that man should worship Him in Spirit and in Truth. It is with this intention that God made covenants. Covenant is a mutual agreement. Testament can also be called Covenant. Testament comes into effect after the death of a person for disposition of his property.

## CONDITIONAL AND UNCONDITIONAL COVENANTS

Covenant between God and Man can be unconditional or conditional. Abrahamic Covenant was unconditional but Mosaic Covenant was conditional. Abrahamic covenant is recorded in Genesis 15:18-21. God made three speeches as we read in Genesis chapter 12, chapter 15 and chapter 17. In Chapters 12 and 15 God made His Will known to Abraham whose name was "Abram" before he was blessed.

In Chapter 17 God asks Abraham that every male child of his seed should be circumcised. Mosaic covenant is seen in Exodus Chapters 19-24. Mosaic covenant is conditional. There is a clause "IF" in this covenant. If Israel was obedient to the covenant they were blessed, and if not they were chastised.

Hebrew Strong's definition number for covenant is 1285. Transliterated word is Bereeth B@riyth pronounced as ber-eeth'.

Greek Strong's definition number for covenant is 1242. Transliterated word is Diatheke Pronounced as "dee-ath-ay'-kay".

Important three speeches God made to Abraham are:

"Now the LORD had said unto Abram, Get thee out of thy country, and from thy kindred, and from thy father's house, unto a land that I will

Leslie M. John

shew thee: And I will make of thee a great nation, and I will bless thee, and make thy name great; and thou shalt be a blessing: And I will bless them that bless thee, and curse him that curseth thee: and in thee shall all families of the earth be blessed". (Genesis 12:1-3)

"In the same day the LORD made a covenant with Abram, saying, Unto thy seed have I given this land, from the river of Egypt unto the great river, the river Euphrates: The Kenites, and the Kenizzites, and the Kadmonites, And the Hittites, and the Perizzites, and the Rephaims, And the Amorites, and the Canaanites, and the Girgashites, and the Jebusites". (Genesis 15:18-21)

"And I will establish my covenant between me and thee and thy seed after thee in their generations for an everlasting covenant, to be a God unto thee, and to thy seed after thee. And I will give unto thee, and to thy seed after thee, the land wherein thou art a stranger, all the land of Canaan, for an everlasting possession; and I will be their God. And God said unto Abraham, Thou shalt keep my covenant therefore, thou, and thy seed after thee in their generations. This is my covenant, which ye shall keep, between me and you and thy seed after thee; Every man child among you shall be circumcised. And ye shall circumcise the flesh of your foreskin; and it shall be a token of the covenant betwixt me and you". (Genesis 17:7-11)

Few verses from the Mosaic Covenant where Hebrew word 'bereeth" was used are:

Ex 19:5 - Now therefore, if ye will obey my voice indeed, and keep my covenant, then ye shall be a peculiar treasure unto me above all people: for all the earth is mine:

And the Ten Commandments as recorded in: Exodus Chapter 20:3-17

In addition:

Ex 23:32 - Thou shalt make no covenant with them, nor with their gods.

Ex 24:7 - And he took the book of the covenant, and read in the audience

Leslie M. John

of the people: and they said, All that the LORD hath said will we do, and be obedient.

Ex 24:8 - And Moses took the blood, and sprinkled it on the people, and said, Behold the blood of the covenant, which the LORD hath made with you concerning all these words.

Some of the important verses where Greek transliterated word "diatheses" was used in the New Testament are as follows:

"Likewise also the cup after supper, saying, This cup is the new testament in my blood, which is shed for you". (Luke 22:20)

"After the same manner also he took the cup, when he had supped, saying, This cup is the new testament in my blood: this do ye, as oft as ye drink it, in remembrance of me". (1 Corinthians 11:25)

Under the Old Covenant those who were under Mosaic Law worshipped God in the Tabernacle according to the instructions as given by God through Moses to Aaron the High Priest.

## PRIESTS

Priests and the High Priests offered animal sacrifices and offerings. Those sacrifices and offerings, more specifically, of Sin Offering, Guilt Offering and Burnt Offerings that were offered on the "Day of Atonement" once a year by the High Priest, as detailed in Leviticus Chapter 16 were the shadows of the substance that was fulfilled in Lord Jesus Christ, who became the sacrifice on behalf of us, entered into the very presence of the Father with His own blood shed on the cross of Calvary.

## LORD JESUS CHRIST THE HIGH PRIEST

Lord Jesus is our High Priest and mediator, who gave us the New Covenant, which is better covenant than the Old Covenant. When the New Covenant was given the Old Covenant became obsolete..

Taking part in the Lord's Supper does not save a person from his sin but it reminds him of the sufferings of Jesus who died for him. But it makes a believer stand in awe before God and worship him in spirit and in truth.

And to Jesus the mediator of the new covenant, and to the blood of sprinkling, that speaketh better things than that of Abel. (Hebrews 12:24)

God made covenant with Adam, Noah, Israel and David.

The Old Covenant, which is the Mosaic Law, was applicable only to Israel. In the Old Testament the Mosaic Law was written on stone but in the New Testament God writes His Laws in hearts. The Old Covenant was restricted to Israel but the New Covenant is extended to all those who accept Jesus as their personal Savior. The mediator of Old Covenant was Moses and the mediator of New Covenant is Lord Jesus Christ.

New Testament believers cannot take part in the Mosaic covenant made to bring the "House of Israel" and the "House of Judah" together. However, Galatians 3:7 records "Know ye therefore that they which are of faith, the same are the children of Abraham".

Jeremiah Chapter 31:31-33 read "Behold, the days come, saith the LORD, that I will make a new covenant with the house of Israel, and with the house of Judah: Not according to the covenant that I made with their fathers in the day that I took them by the hand to bring them out of the land of Egypt; which my covenant they brake, although I was an husband unto them, saith the LORD: But this shall be the covenant that I will make with the house of Israel; After those days, saith the LORD, I will put my law in their inward parts, and write it in their hearts; and will be their God, and they shall be my people".

Hebrews 8:9-10 reads "Not according to the covenant that I made with their fathers in the day when I took them by the hand to lead them out of the land of Egypt; because they continued not in my covenant, and I regarded them not, saith the Lord. For this is the covenant that I will make with the house of Israel after those days, saith the Lord; I will put my laws into their mind, and write them in their hearts: and I will be to them a God, and they shall be to me a people"

Leslie M. John

As the Jews refused to accept Jesus as 'Messiah' the Gentiles had the privilege to enter into His presence. We did not become partakers of the covenant to become one with the House of Israel and/or House of Judah, but we have become partakers of the New Covenant to become the members of His body.

# THE BRIDE

The Church is the bride of Christ, and those who have accepted Jesus as their personal Savior constitute the bride of Christ and in this Church there is no difference between the Jew and Gentile. "For there is no difference between the Jew and the Greek: for the same Lord over all is rich unto all that call upon him. For whosoever shall call upon the name of the Lord shall be saved". (Romans 10:12-13). About Jews Apostle Paul says in Romans 11:25 "Their eyes are blinded to the truth of the Gospel of Jesus Christ". The Church is going to be caught up when Lord Jesus comes again (1 Thessalonians 4:16-17).

What a privilege we have in Jesus that we have become heirs according to the promise given to Abraham. Believers in Christ do not become one like Israel nor do they need to become like Jews but they are greater than those unbelieving Jews. It is not the desire of God to make the believers in Christ to make them like Jews but He desires them to emulate Jesus and worship God.

The New Covenant does not point in the direction of inheriting the blessings to become one with the "House of Israel" and "House of Judah". Gentiles who have accepted Jesus as personal savior have greater privileges than them.

Israel was divided into two kingdoms after King Solomon. The Northern Kingdom was ruled by Jeroboam and the Southern Kingdom by Rehoboam. Both these houses were always at war with each other. The Northern Kingdom was called the "House of Israel" and the Southern Kingdom was called the "House of Judah".

Leslie M. John

# THE PERFECT REDEMPTION

The perfect redemption from sin is only through the sacrifice of Jesus who died on behalf of every one. He is the Salvation and there is no other way to obtain salvation. It is evident from the Scriptures that everything that was under the 'law' required purging through the blood and there was no purification of sins unless blood was shed.

The shedding of the blood of the bulls and goats and the placing of ashes of burnt heifer outside the camp or the sprinkling of the blood of unclean bulls could separate the sinners unto salvation; but these acts never provided the ultimate redemption from sin until the blood of the Son of God, Lord Jesus Christ, was shed upon the cross of Calvary for everyone. The blood of Jesus shed cleanses from all sin and it was the perfect sacrifice for receiving salvation.

We read in Numbers Chapter 19 the details about the ordinance of the law which required a red heifer without any spot on it, without any blemish and upon which never any yoke was put on was brought for sacrifice and given to priest Eleazar. The priest was then to take her blood with his finger and sprinkle it directly before the tabernacle of the congregation seven times.

"And one shall burn the heifer in his sight; her skin, and her flesh, and her blood, with her dung, shall he burn" (Numbers 19:5)

One had to burn the heifer in his sight. The heifer had to be burnt with its skin, her flesh, and blood and with her dung. The priest had to take cedar wood, and hyssop, and scarlet, and cast it into the midst of the burning of the heifer. Hyssop is a plant whose leaves have an aromatic smell and pungent taste.

A man who is clean was to gather up the ashes of the heifer and lay them outside the camp in a clean place for congregation of the children of Israel for what is called as "water of separation" and that was 'purification of sins'.

Leslie M. John

There is no greater message in the Bible than that of God reconciling man unto Himself and sending His one and only begotten Son to be crucified for the remission of our sins. All those who believe in Lord Jesus Christ will be saved and have everlasting life. Lord Jesus Christ told us that as often as we eat the bread and drink the cup at the Lord's Supper we do show forth his death until he comes (1 Corinthians 11:26).

As the Lord's Supper reminds us of his sufferings and death, and resurrection reminds us his triumph over Satan we are duty bound to participate in the Lord's Supper if we love him. Keep aside all negative interpretations and do participate in the Lord's Supper. The shed blood of Jesus is available for cleansing anyone's sin provided the sinner confesses his sins to Him and accepts Him as his personal Savior.

The presence of blemish in the shed blood of bulls and goats made it not a perfect sacrifice. But, the blood of Jesus Christ, who through the eternal Spirit offered himself, was without any blemish. The blood of Jesus purges our conscience from dead works to serve the living God.

When Moses spoke to the children of Israel every precept according to the law, he said, that the blood of the calves and of goats with water, and scarlet wool, and hyssop which he sprinkled upon the book and the people, became the testament. This was done under the authority of God. Moses sprinkled not only upon the book of law and the people, but he sprinkled upon the tabernacle and all the vessels of the ministry.

Thus the sacrifice of animals was done to separate them unto salvation but the salvation is only through Lord Jesus Christ. Under that dispensation the grace of God was veiled but the same grace is revealed unto us now and we see this in our lives as in a glass (2 Cor.3:18).

The high priest went into the 'most holy' of the tabernacle once every year, and he never did so before he offered the blood for himself first and for the sins of the people next.

This ceremonial law could not make anyone perfect nor did such observances of law could make anyone enter into heaven. Christ was once offered to bear the sins of many. It was a perfect sacrifice and it was

Leslie M. John

done once and for all. Jesus, by such offering, destroyed the works of the devil.

The believers in Lord Jesus Christ shall be made holy. The veil of the temple was rent into two from top to the bottom when Jesus was hung up on that cursed and rugged cross opening the way for us to enter into the 'Most Holy'. (Heb. 9:28 and Matt.27:51)

God who said, "they shall be my people" in Jeremiah 31:31 said in Hosea Chapter 1 that because the House of Israel have rebelled against God's commandments, they are not His people (Lo-Ammi). God had compassion on the House of Judah.

Later in Hosea Chapter 2:14-23 God makes reconciliatory pronouncements. In the New Testament God says again that "they shall be my people".

"But this shall be the covenant that I will make with the house of Israel; After those days, saith the LORD, I will put my law in their inward parts, and write it in their hearts; and will be their God, and they shall be my people" (Jeremiah 31:33)

In the Millennial rule of Lord Jesus Christ the 'House of Israel' and the 'House of Judah' will be united and that will be the fulfillment of the "New Covenant" prophesied in Jeremiah 31:1-34.

We the members of the "Body of Christ" whose head the Lord Jesus Christ, are in Church and have gained the blessings of the "New Covenant" already. This is the Grace of God that even though we are Gentiles God has placed us far above the Jews. We have inherited the spiritual blessings to become "One New Man" consisting of the Jews and Gentiles in the Church and have heavenly blessings.

This was the mystery Apostle Paul spoke of in Ephesians Chapter 3:3 and Ephesians Chapter 3:6.

God delivered us from the power of darkness, and translated us into the kingdom of his dear Son Lord Jesus Christ.

Leslie M. John

"Who hath delivered us from the power of darkness, and hath translated us into the kingdom of his dear Son" (Colossians 1:13)

Blessings and Covenants are given to Israel and we the Gentiles, who were strangers to the Blessings and Covenants, have already been blessed with greater blessings than that of the Israel, who are promised with earthly blessings. We have been forgiven of our sins, and are assured to be with the Lord for ever and ever.

The Church is the bride of Lord Jesus Christ will be 'caught up' to be with him for ever and ever. The prophesy in Ezekiel Chapter 37 will be fulfilled in future when the 'House of Israel' and the 'House of Judah' will be united by God and then they will have earthly blessings.

"And he is the head of the body, the church: who is the beginning, the firstborn from the dead; that in all things he might have the preeminence". (Colossians 1:18)

And what agreement hath the temple of God with idols? for ye are the temple of the living God; as God hath said, I will dwell in them, and walk in them; and I will be their God, and they shall be my people. (2 Corinthians 6:16)

Galatians Chapter 3:6, 7, 14 and 29 read: "Even as Abraham believed God, and it was accounted to him for righteousness. Know ye therefore that they which are of faith, the same are the children of Abraham. That the blessing of Abraham might come on the Gentiles through Jesus Christ; that we might receive the promise of the Spirit through faith. And if ye be Christ's, then are ye Abraham's seed, and heirs according to the promise".

Jesus Christ by shedding his own blood has become our mediator and high priest. We do not need any priest or mediator other than Jesus to approach the Father and enter into His Holy Presence. Confessing sins to human priests is a gross error.

Lord Jesus Christ, who said, "this do in remembrance of me" is alone worthy of our worship in spirit and in truth. Let us, therefore, as often as

Leslie M. John

possible, "do in remembrance of" of him, whose blood cleansed our sins and made us partakers of the blessings that belonged to Israel.

"For I have received of the Lord that which also I delivered unto you, That the Lord Jesus the same night in which he was betrayed took bread: And when he had given thanks, he brake it, and said, Take, eat: this is my body, which is broken for you: this do in remembrance of me. After the same manner also he took the cup, when he had supped, saying, This cup is the new testament in my blood: this do ye, as oft as ye drink it, in remembrance of me.

For as often as ye eat this bread, and drink this cup, ye do shew the Lord's death till he come". (1 Corinthians 11:23-26)

The writer of Hebrews refers to the Old Covenant and the New Covenant in Hebrews Chapter 8.

"For finding fault with them, he saith, Behold, the days come, saith the Lord, when I will make a new covenant with the house of Israel and with the house of Judah" (Hebrews 8:8)

"In that he saith, A new covenant, he hath made the first old. Now that which decayeth and waxeth old is ready to vanish away. (Hebrews 8:13)

"And to Jesus the mediator of the new covenant, and to the blood of sprinkling, that speaketh better things than that of Abel" (Hebrews 12:24)

## GLORIFIED STATUS

"Now therefore why tempt ye God, to put a yoke upon the neck of the disciples, which neither our fathers nor we were able to bear?" (Acts 15:10)

Who would want an inferior position that is earned through hard struggle when an exalted position is available easily? It is similar to this when Jews prefer to follow the Old Testament provisions while God has provided an easy method of procuring heavenly blessings through Lord

Leslie M. John

Jesus Christ. The Father gives to all those who are predestined to be confirmed to be in the image of His Son, glorified bodies, who rule from New Jerusalem that comes down from heaven. All those who are left-behind will be in earthly bodies on this earth to be ruled over.

It is as simple as accepting Lord Jesus Christ as personal Savior by confessing sins to Him. Those who will be caught up into mid-air to meet Lord Jesus Christ when He comes for His bride will be in the glorified bodies conformed to the image of Christ. Lord Jesus Christ with His bride, the Church, the body of Christ, steps on to the mount olives and then after 'Sheep and Goat' judgment the Lord will rule over those who are on this earth. The reign will be for thousand years. What a privilege is being lost by those who are   called as "My People" by God that they are choosing to be on the earth with earthly bodies to be ruled over by Lord Jesus Christ and those that are confirmed to the image of Him.

"For the Lord himself shall descend from heaven with a shout, with the voice of the archangel, and with the trump of God: and the dead in Christ shall rise first: Then we which are alive and remain shall be caught up together with them in the clouds, to meet the Lord in the air: and so shall we ever be with the Lord". (1 Thessalonians 4:16-17)

"Behold, I shew you a mystery; We shall not all sleep, but we shall all be changed, In a moment, in the twinkling of an eye, at the last trump: for the trumpet shall sound, and the dead shall be raised incorruptible, and we shall be changed. For this corruptible must put on incorruption, and this mortal must put on immortality. So when this corruptible shall have put on incorruption, and this mortal shall have put on immortality, then shall be brought to pass the saying that is written, Death is swallowed up in victory" (1 Corinthians 15:51-54)

"For whom he did foreknow, he also did predestinate to be conformed to the image of his Son, that he might be the firstborn among many brethren". (Romans 8:29)

Leslie M. John

# CHAPTER 7
# GOSPEL OF GRACE

The Gospel of Grace was preached during Acts Period and many Gentiles were saved during Acts period. After Death, Burial and Resurrection of Lord Jesus Christ, He did not wait until Acts period to be completed for message of salvation to be sent to Gentiles nor did He instruct Apostle Paul to take the message of Salvation until after Acts 28:28 was written.

The Book of Acts contains historical facts of Apostles, primarily that Apostle Peter and Apostle Paul. The Book of Acts contains the historical transition of the "Kingdom" message to the message of 'One New Man" the "CHURCH", whose head is Lord Jesus Christ with members from Jews and Gentiles.

The transition could be seen from:

1. Preaching of Gospel in Jerusalem ("And the word of God increased; and the number of the disciples multiplied in Jerusalem greatly; and a great company of the priests were obedient to the faith" Acts 6:7)

2. Preaching of Gospel in Judea and Samaria ("Then had the churches rest throughout all Judaea and Galilee and Samaria, and were edified; and walking in the fear of the Lord, and in the comfort of the Holy Ghost, were multiplied". Acts 9:31)

3. Preaching of Gospel in Tyre and Sidon (Herod was smitten by God and the Church is blessed. "But the word of God grew and multiplied". Acts 12:20-24)

4. Preaching of Gospel in Asia Minor ("And so were the churches established in the faith, and increased in number daily" Acts 16:5)

5. Preaching of Gospel in Europe ("And this was known to all the Jews and Greeks also dwelling at Ephesus; and fear fell on them all, and the name of the Lord Jesus was magnified" Acts 19:17) and 6. Preaching the

Page 84

Leslie M. John

Gospel in Europe:

(a) "Be it known therefore unto you, that the salvation of God is sent unto the Gentiles, and [that] they will hear it" Acts 28:28

(b) "Preaching the kingdom of God, and teaching those things which concern the Lord Jesus Christ, with all confidence, no man forbidding him" Acts 28:31)

Some have made a big deal differentiating Acts 28:28 and Acts 28:31 and misinterpreted Grafting which Paul spoke of in Romans Chapters 9-11. The Gentles saved during Acts period were not circumcised to become proselytes. In Christ circumcised and un-circumcised are all equal members of the Church. Peter, James, Mark, Paul and Barnabas were as much equal members of the Church as any other Gentile, who believed in Jesus Christ as his/her personal Savior. If it is argued that there is no Church during Acts period, then it goes to say that Peter and Paul were also not members of the "Body of Christ".

"Having abolished in his flesh the enmity, even the law of commandments contained in ordinances; for to make in himself of twain one new man, so making peace" (Ephesians 2:15)

Let us read two verses before we go into the details of the "one new man". The phrase "new man" has different meaning than that of "one new man".

"And that ye put on the new man, which after God is created in righteousness and true holiness". (Ephesians 4:24)

"And have put on the new man, which is renewed in knowledge after the image of him that created him" (Colossians 3:10)

Those verses in Ephesians 4:24 and Colossians 3:10 point towards the one who has accepted Lord Jesus Christ as personal savior and become 'new man' having put off the old man in him. He is a new creation in Christ Jesus. God considers him as righteous and holy. He is renewed in the knowledge of God who created him.

Leslie M. John

The phrase "one new man" referred to in Ephesians 2:15 is the one body of Christ that has members from Jews and Gentiles. They are made one in Christ and there is no difference between them.

There are few conditions that need to have been fulfilled before 'one new man' came into existence. Firstly, the condition "Having abolished in his flesh the enmity, even the law of commandments contained in ordinances" should have been fulfilled. Secondly, the one becoming part of that "one new man" should have been cleansed of his sin through the blood of Lord Jesus Christ. That is to say the person who becomes a member of that 'one new man' should have repented of his/her sin and accepted Lord Jesus Christ as his/her personal Savior. Then, obviously the 'one new man' also can be called member of the "Church", "the body of Christ" and the "Bride of Christ". Thirdly, the condition "to make in himself of twain" should have been fulfilled.

## THE FIRST CONDITION

Was it after Acts 28:28 or is it when Jesus was crucified on the cross? Obviously, the condition was fulfilled when Jesus was crucified on the cross.

"Jesus, when he had cried again with a loud voice, yielded up the ghost". (Matthew 27:50)

The veil in the Temple was rent into two from top to bottom, opening the way from Holy to the Holies and earth did quake and rocks rent. (Matthew 27:51)

The centurion and others who were with him, watching Jesus saw the earthquake and things that have happened at that time and greatly feared and acknowledged that Jesus was the "Son of God" (Matthew 27:54)

Jesus rose from the dead on the third day (Matthew 28:6), and after forty days he ascended into heaven and will come back again in the same manner he ascended into heaven. (Acts 1:9-11)

Leslie M. John

## THE SECOND CONDITION

Bible says we all, irrespective of whether we are Jews or Gentiles, have sinned and come short of the glory of God (Romans 3:9, 23) and the wages of sin is death but the gift of God is eternal life through Jesus Christ our Lord. (Romans 6:23)

To become partakers of God's blessing and to receive salvation one has to repent of his/her sins and accept Jesus Christ as personal savior. Bible says:

"That if thou shalt confess with thy mouth the Lord Jesus, and shalt believe in thine heart that God hath raised him from the dead, thou shalt be saved" (Romans 10:9)

"If we confess our sins, he is faithful and just to forgive us our sins, and to cleanse us from all unrighteousness". (1 John 1:9)

## THE THIRD CONDITION

Whoever has accepted Lord Jesus Christ as his personal savior, whether we be Jews or Gentiles, whether we be bond or free, have been made to drink of one spirit and for by one Spirit we are all baptized into one body. (1 Corinthians 12:13)

## JESUS BECAME OUR HIGH PRIEST

"For we have not an high priest which cannot be touched with the feeling of our infirmities; but was in all points tempted like as we are, yet without sin". (Hebrews 4:15)

The barrier between Jews and Gentiles was removed. That is to say, the provision for 'one new man' was made immediately when Jesus was crucified on the cross. Now the question is when exactly the Jews and Gentiles became one. Was it after Acts 28:28 or is it when Jesus was crucified on the cross?

When the day of Pentecost was fully come as we read in Acts Chapter2

Leslie M. John

there were in Jerusalem Jews, devout men, out of every nation under heaven.

"And there were dwelling at Jerusalem Jews, devout men, out of every nation under heaven". (Acts 2:5)

Also in Acts 2:9-11 there is a mention of all those who were present from different regions.

"Parthians, and Medes, and Elamites, and the dwellers in Mesopotamia, and in Judaea, and Cappadocia, in Pontus, and Asia, Phrygia, and Pamphylia, in Egypt, and in the parts of Libya about Cyrene, and strangers of Rome, Jews and proselytes, Cretes and Arabians, we do hear them speak in our tongues the wonderful works of God". (Acts 2:9-11)

The people present there when Peter spoke of Jesus starting from Acts 2:14 were from Judea and from those who dwell at Jerusalem. Note how the scriptures clearly distinguish those who were present in Jerusalem as from "Judea" and "all ye that dwell at Jerusalem". If only Jews were there at that time, the distinction should not have been made, but the scriptures clearly distinguish two categories of people present at the time when Peter spoke about Jesus of Nazareth.

Those who were present in Jerusalem during the time of Pentecost were empowered to speak about Lord Jesus Christ. Holy Spirit, who is the "Promise of the Father", came upon all those who were commanded by Lord Jesus Christ to wait at Jerusalem until Holy Spirit came upon them. Acts 2:4 says:

"And they were all filled with the Holy Ghost, and began to speak with other tongues, as the Spirit gave them utterance".

When this news was heard abroad, multitudes came together and were confused because every man heard them speak in his own language and they all understood one another. They were all amazed and marvelled and said to each other, "...Behold, are not all these which speak Galilaeans? And how hear we every man in our own tongue, wherein we were born?" (Acts 2:1-8)

Paul quotes Hosea Chapter 1 and says in Romans 9:25 that those Israelites who were unfaithful to God were called "Not my people" by

Leslie M. John

God. They were all Gentiles. But what about those who were not the descendants of Jacob, who were present in Jerusalem at the time when Peter spoke of Jesus? Were there no Roman Government officials? How sure is anyone to say that those who were called "Parthians, and Medes, and Elamites, and the dwellers in Mesopotamia, and in Judaea, and Cappadocia, in Pontus, and Asia, Phrygia, and Pamphylia, in Egypt, and in the parts of Libya about Cyrene, and strangers of Rome, Jews and proselytes, Cretes and Arabians" were also the descendants of Jacob.

I Chronicles Chapter 1: 17-28 have the details of sons of Shem, Elamites, and many others. Neither scriptures nor the history records of Flavius Josephus show that all those were descendants of Jacob. They were all Gentiles. There is no basis to say that those three thousand saved when Peter preached were only Jews or descendants of Jacob. There are some who say without producing any evidence that they were mixed generations from Jacob's descendants and pure Gentiles and there are some who say that they were all from "House of Israel" who mixed up with Samaritans without showing where those from "House of Israel" were or are now. Some try to make up some stories even from those narrations which are mystery.

"Then they that gladly received his word were baptized: and the same day there were added unto them about three thousand souls". (Acts 2:41)

Later many more souls from Jews and Gentiles were added to the Church.

"Praising God, and having favour with all the people. And the Lord added to the church daily such as should be saved" (Acts 2:47)

Leslie M. John

# CHAPTER 8
# GREAT COMMISSION

"**G**o ye therefore, and teach all nations, baptizing them in the name of the Father, and of the Son, and of the Holy Ghost: Teaching them to observe all things whatsoever I have commanded you: and, lo, I am with you alway, even unto the end of the world. Amen" (Matthew 28:19-20)

The term "Great Commission" does not appear in the Bible, but just as we use few words/phrases in Christian common parlance to communicate certain meanings of the words like "Trinity", "Millennium", "Rapture", and "Bema Seat of Christ" the phrase "Great Commission" is used to convey the meaning that Jesus commanded his disciples to preach the Gospel. There are four passages where we see the commandment of Jesus to preach the Gospel. Reading through Mark 16:15-18 some interpret that the commission given to the disciples is already fulfilled and that there is no commission in the present age to preach the Gospel. Their argument is that the Word of God in itself is sufficient for someone to understand the Scriptures and no preaching is necessary. Their argument is that the disciples were asked to preach the Gospel and signs followed such preaching, and, since there are no signs followed in the present age the commission that was given in Matthew Chapter 28:18-20 is not valid. New Testament Church took birth as we read in Acts Chapter 2.

KINGDOM OF GOD

Jesus preached that the kingdom of God was at hand and the disciples who were sent two by two preached that men should repent. "And they went out, and preached that men should repent. And they cast out many devils, and anointed with oil many that were sick, and healed them" (Mark 6:12-13)

The disciples of Lord Jesus Christ preached the Gospel of Jesus Christ only after they were empowered to speak with the power of Holy Spirit.

Leslie M. John

(Acts 1:4 & 8). Later, Apostle Paul was chosen to preach the Gospel to Gentiles. Paul's ministry was basically intended for Gentiles, but the commission he received did not restrict him preaching to Jews in the beginning.

"But the Lord said unto him, Go thy way: for he is a chosen vessel unto me, to bear my name before the Gentiles, and kings, and the children of Israel" (Acts 9:15)

In fact, he preached to Jews and when they rejected him he went with message of salvation to Gentiles. This does not mean the Church came into existence after Acts 28:28.

After the ascension of Jesus and as the disciples were waiting they received the power to speak about Jesus. Earlier the disciples preached according to their knowledge thinking about the earthly kingdom of God. The disciples of Lord Jesus asked him as to when the kingdom would be restored to Israel but then Jesus said to them it was not for them to know the times and seasons which the Father had put in his own power.

John said: "John answered them, saying, I baptize with water: but there standeth one among you, whom ye know not". John 1:26
Mar 1:8 I indeed have baptized you with water: but he shall baptize you with the Holy Ghost.

## GOSPEL MESSAGES

Bible speaks of Gospel, which is the good news of the Lord Jesus Christ's bearing sin of mankind, His resurrection and ascension. This Gospel is preached in different forms and perspectives. There four different forms:

1. The Gospel of the 'Kingdom of God' that deals with the fulfillment of Davidic covenant, The 'kingdom shall be established for ever before thee: thy throne shall be established for ever'. (2 Samuel 7:16). This Kingdom of God includes the thousand year literal reign of Lord Jesus Christ from the throne of David in Jerusalem, as detailed in Zechariah 14:9 "And the LORD shall be king over all the earth: in that day shall

Leslie M. John

there be one LORD, and his name one"

2. The 'Gospel of Christ' deals with the Salvation of mankind that Apostle Paul spoke of, as the 'Grace of God', that Jesus died for our sins, and that He was raised from the dead. Jesus died and was raised for our justification and we are justified because of our belief in Him. "For we stretch not ourselves beyond our measure, as though we reached not unto you: for we are come as far as to you also in preaching the gospel of Christ" (2 Corinthians 10:14)

3. The 'Gospel' that is called 'everlasting gospel', preached unto those, who did not believe in him, and who will pass through the 'great tribulation' until the last days before the last judgment. "And I said unto him, Sir, thou knowest. And he said to me, These are they which came out of great tribulation, and have washed their robes, and made them white in the blood of the Lamb". (Revelation 7:14)

4. The Gospel that is called 'another gospel', which is the perversion of the Gospel of Christ. Christians are warned to be careful about this 'another gospel' by the agents of Satan, who transforms himself as the angel of light. Apostle Paul writes about this gospel. "I marvel that ye are so soon removed from him that called you into the grace of Christ unto another gospel: Which is not another; but there be some that trouble you, and would pervert the gospel of Christ". (Galatians 1:6-7). False apostles calling themselves as apostles of Christ preach this gospel perverting the truth of the real gospel of Jesus that Apostle Paul calls as 'my gospel' in Romans 2:16, the gospel of Christ. However, "my gospel" is not to be understood as Paul's personal Gospel, but it is the same Gospel which Peter and others preached; that is of Lord Jesus Christ's death, burial and resurrection. Paul was contradicting those who were Judaizers, who insisted on circumcision for Gentiles to be saved.

This 'another gospel' dispels the efficacy of the blood of Jesus Christ and gives importance to law and works associated with it. This gospel seeks to add works to faith in Christ. It shows that mere faith in Jesus is not enough to be saved but good works need to be done. While good works follow salvation, they are not conditional for receiving salvation.

Leslie M. John

Paul writes to the Church in Thessalonica that when they received the word of God, which they heard it from him, they received it not as the word of men, but as the truth from the word of God. He says that the truth of the Gospel will lead them to repent of their sins and help them to believe in Jesus Christ. (1 Thessalonians 2:13)

## COMMISSION IN MARK 16:15-18

It would be good to ponder on Mark 16:15-18 before Matthew 28:18-20 is taken into consideration. The preceding verse of Mark 16:15 is about Lord Jesus Christ appearing to his disciples as they sat at meal and reproach them on their unbelief and hardness of heart. The disciples obviously did not believe those things that had come to pass after the resurrection of Lord Jesus Christ. After the resurrection Jesus appeared to Mary Magdalene, from whom Jesus had cast away seven devils (Luke 8:2 and Mark 16:9).

It was not to the Virgin Mary that Jesus appeared first but it was to this sinner woman who was redeemed by Jesus that he appeared first. There is a great comfort in knowing that Jesus has concern for sinners and for their redemption. The subsequent verses after Mark 16:18 say that Lord Jesus Christ was received up into heaven and sat on the right hand of Majesty on high. The disciples went forth and preached the Gospel everywhere. Notice the word 'everywhere'. It does not confine to the regions of Jerusalem.

As they preached the Gospel the signs followed them. The signs were casting out devils, speaking in tongues, taking up serpents and that poison would not hurt them. Also, they shall lay hands on the sick who will recover, obviously meaning that they would be healed. (Mark 16:15-18)

The reason why some Christians say that there is no commission now is based on their belief that there are no such signs followed after preaching. Here, we should remember that it was after resurrection when Lord Jesus Christ gave instructions that he said such signs will follow after preaching. But then, this commission in Mark 16:15-18 was

Leslie M. John

intended for preaching to Gentiles. That message was only to Jews.

"An army chaplain once said to the Duke of Wellington, 'Do you think that it is of any use our taking the gospel to the hill tribes in India? Will they ever receive it?' The duke replied, 'What are your marching orders?' That was the only answer he gave. Stern disciplinarian as that great soldier was, he only wanted marching orders, and he obeyed; and he meant that every soldier of the cross must obey the marching orders of Christ, his great Commander." (Spurgeon)

Those who know about rules in the Armed forces will appreciate what Spurgeon was saying. Go forward without looking at the consequences. Marching orders are to go ahead; no questioning. Some of Christians are out there now who say signs ceased so also the commission ceased. They say there is no 'Great Commission'.

## BEFORE THE CRUCIFIXION OF JESUS

The commandment that Jesus gave to the disciples before he was crucified was in Matthew 10:5 "These twelve Jesus sent forth, and commanded them, saying, Go not into the way of the Gentiles, and into any city of the Samaritans enter ye not".

## AFTER THE CRUCIFIXION OF JESUS

"But ye shall receive power, after that the Holy Ghost is come upon you: and ye shall be witnesses unto me both in Jerusalem, and in all Judaea, and in Samaria, and unto the uttermost part of the earth". (Acts 1:8). Notice the phrase "after the Holy Ghost is come upon you". Acts 1:8 shows that the disciples were ordained to be the witnesses of Lord Jesus Christ first in Jerusalem, then in Judea and Samaria, and then in uttermost part of the earth. The commission here says that the order of their being witnesses should be first among Jews in the regions of Jerusalem, and then in Judea and Samaria, which are the regions where Jews mixed up with Gentiles and then lastly to the uttermost parts of the earth, which means that they should be his disciples among the Gentiles in the uttermost part of the earth.

## JEWS ONLY DURING PENTECOST?

It was feast time and there were men from every nation under heaven. The text in the following verses does not show that these all men were circumcised Proselytes.

Acts 2:5 And there were dwelling at Jerusalem Jews, devout men, out of every nation under heaven.

Acts 2:6 Now when this was noised abroad, the multitude came together, and were confounded, because that every man heard them speak in his own language.

Acts 2:7 And they were all amazed and marvelled, saying one to another, Behold, are not all these which speak Galilaeans?

Acts 2:8 And how hear we every man in our own tongue, wherein we were born?

Acts 2:9 Parthians, and Medes, and Elamites, and the dwellers in Mesopotamia, and in Judaea, and Cappadocia, in Pontus, and Asia,

Acts 2:10 Phrygia, and Pamphylia, in Egypt, and in the parts of Libya about Cyrene, and strangers of Rome, Jews and proselytes,

Acts 2:11 Cretes and Arabians, we do hear them speak in our tongues the wonderful works of God.

Acts 2:12 And they were all amazed, and were in doubt, saying one to another, What meaneth this?

Acts 2:13 Others mocking said, These men are full of new wine.

## SEQUENCE OF PREACHING

The Word of God divides the sequence of preaching into three, that is, first in Jerusalem, second in Judea and Samaria and third in the uttermost part of the earth. We see the three stages in Acts from

Leslie M. John

Chapters 1-7, second from Chapters 8 to 12 and third from Chapters 13 to 28. The best possible sources identify that all the epistles of Paul were written during the time-period mentioned in Acts of Apostles. In fact the Book of Acts does not record all the acts of all the disciples. This book mainly concentrates on some of the acts of Apostle Paul and some of the Acts of Peter. The Chronology of the epistles and the dates when they were written are disputable.

## JESUS IS THE EXPRESS IMAGE OF THE FATHER

 Hebrews 1:3 confirms that Lord Jesus Christ is the brightness of the Father and express image of His person, and upholds everything by the word of his power. He purged our sins and sat down on the right hand of the Majesty on high.
 The argument of those who say that there is no Commission left in the present age is also based on these verses:
Acts 10:28, Acts 11:19-20, Gal.2:7-9, James 1:1

## CORNELIEUS A GENTILE SAVED

It is worth considering each verse in its context. The whole Chapter 10 of Acts is about the Salvation provided for a Gentile named Cornelius. There are disputes in interpretations as to whether Cornelius was already a believer and Holy Spirit fell on him while Peter was yet speaking to him or he believed Jesus when Peter spoke to him and then the Holy Spirit fell on him.

## HOLY SPIRIT CAME UPON THEM

"While Peter yet spake these words, the Holy Ghost fell on all them which heard the word" (Acts 10:44)

 Cornelius was just man who gave alms yet the angel of the Lord desired of him that he should be spoken to of the message of crucifixion and resurrection of Jesus signifying that his belief that being a just man and giving alms would not save him. After Cornelius heard this message Holy Spirit fell on not only on him but all them that heard the Gospel of Christ.

Leslie M. John

Marvelous are the ways of God who prepares his followers for his work. There was Cornelius a Gentile in God's sight. Cornelius was a Centurion, who was just, giving alms and living a good life. Bible says no good works will save a person; but only faith in Jesus will save a person. Here is a man who thought that his works are enough to be saved. But then, the angel of the Lord appeared to him in vision and told him that God has considered his alms and accepted his piety but then he should send forth men for calling Peter who was in Joppa and that he will tell Cornelius as to what he should do.

Simon Peter was staying at a tanner's house as recorded in Acts 9:43. A tanner is the one who does tanning and tanning is the process or art of converting skins into leather. Basically the tanner is the one who deals with dead animals. According to Jews one that is dealing with dead animals is abominable. A woman in Jewish community is permitted to divorce her husband if he is involved with dead animals. God was preparing his disciple Peter by allowing him to stay with a person who was dealing with dead animals. Peter was being prepared to approach Gentile Cornelius.

## PETER WAS ASKED NOT TO CALL UNCLEAN

This was the time when Peter had a strange experience. He went up the housetop to pray and was very hungry. He saw heaven opened and a certain vessel that was like a sheet came down with different kinds of four footed animals, fowls and creeping things on it. Peter heard a voice saying to him that he should rise, kill them and eat. Peter was reluctant to eat them as he thought that they were unclean. This happened again, and the voice said to him that those which are considered as clean by God should not be considered as unclean by man. Peter refused to eat and this happened third time and the vessel taken up into heaven.

"But Peter said, Not so, Lord; for I have never eaten any thing that is common or unclean. And the voice spake unto him again the second time, What God hath cleansed, that call not thou common". (Acts 10:14-15)

Leslie M. John

"And he said unto them, Ye know how that it is an unlawful thing for a man that is a Jew to keep company, or come unto one of another nation; but God hath shewed me that I should not call any man common or unclean". (Acts 10:28)

When Peter was thinking that it was a vision, there came men from Cornelius inquiring about Peter. The Spirit of the Lord said to Peter that he should go to Cornelius and he went. Cornelius saw Peter and worshipped him by falling on his feet but then Peter lifted him immediately and said that he was a man like Cornelius. That was to mean that only God is worthy of worship. Peter said to him a man should not call any one as unclean if God has called him as clean.

Peter testified about Jesus of Nazareth who died for all of us, and that God raised him on the third day. As Peter was yet speaking Holy Spirit fell on them and they all marveled. Holy Spirit fell on the Gentiles as well. Please note very carefully the word 'Gentiles' is plural here. That is to say not only Cornelius but other Gentiles were also saved. This also should not be taken as an isolated case to call it as an exception. It was indeed an opening door for Gentiles to receive the Gospel. "And they of the circumcision which believed were astonished, as many as came with Peter, because that on the Gentiles also was poured out the gift of the Holy Ghost". (Acts 10:45)

This is similar to what we see in Acts Chapters 1 and 2. It is wrong to presume that all the three thousand who were added unto them were Jews and it is also wrong to presume that Cornelius was grafted into Good Olive Tree about which Paul wrote in Romans chapters 9 through 11. A Gentile does not need to be grafted into Good Olive Tree and become Jew first and then become the body of Christ. Paul's comparison of Good Olive Tree and grafting of wild Olive branches is misunderstood by some. It is clear that Cornelius was an uncircumcised Gentile.

Apostle Paul's analogy of wild olive branches being grafted into natural olive tree is to mean that the Gentiles are made equal partners in the spiritual blessings along with Jews. Some of the natural branches were cut off because of their unbelief and in their place the wild olive branches are grafted. This is also not to mean that to accommodate

Leslie M. John

Gentiles in the natural olive tree the branches of the natural branches were cut off, but because of their unbelief that the Jews, who are considered as natural olive branches, were cut off.

The wild olive branches are asked not to take pride in themselves because they were grafted into natural olive tree. Paul warns that if natural branches were cut off because of their unbelief, God will not hesitate to cut off wild olive branches. This does not mean that salvation will be lost by any believer in Christ, but it only means that they will be cut off to make way for the natural branches.

Peter was the first one to preach the gospel to Gentiles although Apostle Paul was called to be a minister for Gentiles. True to the words of Jesus who said, upon this rock I will build my Church, Peter was the first one to preach about Jesus of Nazareth in Acts Chapter 2 and Acts Chapter 10

"But ye shall receive power, after that the Holy Ghost is come upon you: and ye shall be witnesses unto me both in Jerusalem, and in all Judaea, and in Samaria, and unto the uttermost part of the earth" (Acts 1:8)

It is also wrong to presume that Jerusalem had only Jews during the period when Jesus was crucified. Roman Government was in itself was not of Jews! In Acts Chapter 2 there is a mention that after the Pentecost was fully come in many people came to Jerusalem out of every nation under heaven.

## HOUSE OF ISRAEL AND HOUSE OF JUDAH

After the captivity of the "House of Israel" and the "House of Judah" by Assyrians and Babylonians there is no evidence that "House of Israel" returned to Israel to contend that those who were in Samaria and other parts of Northern Israel were the seed of Jacob. "And there were dwelling at Jerusalem Jews, devout men, out of every nation under heaven". (Acts 2:5)
Then they that gladly received his word were baptized: and the same day there were added unto them about three thousand souls. (Acts 2:41)

With regard to Acts Chapter 11:19-20 it is true that they began preaching

Leslie M. John

to Jews only in the beginning but then according to verse 20 they spoke to Grecians and "preached the Lord Jesus". That is to say from then onward they preached Lord Jesus to Gentiles as well. Likewise Peter was commissioned to preach to Jews while Apostle Paul was commissioned to preach to Gentiles as recorded in Acts 11:19-20 and in Galatians 2:7-9.

## DID PETER WRITE TO GENTILES?

There is a greater evidence to show that Peter wrote to scattered Jews among Gentile Nations as we read in 1 Peter 1:1 but there is also an opinion that Peter wrote to Gentiles. "Peter, an apostle of Jesus Christ, to the strangers scattered throughout Pontus, Galatia, Cappadocia, Asia, and Bithynia" (1 Peter 1:1). The epistle was written somewhere around AD 60 before the Period of Acts ended in AD 63.

"Who his own self bare our sins in his own body on the tree, that we, being dead to sins, should live unto righteousness: by whose stripes ye were healed". (1 Peter 2:24)

"Forasmuch as ye know that ye were not redeemed with corruptible things, as silver and gold, from your vain conversation received by tradition from your fathers; But with the precious blood of Christ, as of a lamb without blemish and without spot: Who verily was foreordained before the foundation of the world, but was manifest in these last times for you, Who by him do believe in God, that raised him up from the dead, and gave him glory; that your faith and hope might be in God". (1 Peter 1:18-21)

"And being brought on their way by the church, they passed through Phenice and Samaria, declaring the conversion of the Gentiles: and they caused great joy unto all the brethren. And when they were come to Jerusalem, they were received of the church, and [of] the apostles and elders, and they declared all things that God had done with them" Acts 15:3-4

"And when there had been much disputing, Peter rose up, and said unto them, Men [and] brethren, ye know how that a good while ago God made choice among us, that the Gentiles by my mouth should hear the word of the gospel, and believe". Acts 15:7

## JAMES's ADDRESS

James addressed in James 1:1 to the twelve tribes of Israel scattered abroad of their errors. He specifically wrote to the scattered twelve tribes of Israel, but then it was not to mean that Gospel of Jesus Christ was not preached to the Gentiles during that period. There is considerable exhortation to Gentiles in James 5:1-6

## POST-ACTS PERIOD BELIEF

There is inconsistency in believing that Gospel of Jesus Christ was preached by only Apostle Paul to Gentiles based on Acts 28:27 and 28 and to presume that Paul's commission to take the message of salvation to Gentiles commenced after Acts 28:31.

"And upon the first day of the week, when the disciples came together to break bread, Paul preached unto them, ready to depart on the morrow; and continued his speech until midnight". (Acts 20:7)

 And after the uproar was ceased, Paul called unto him the disciples, and embraced them, and departed for to go into Macedonia. And when he had gone over those parts, and had given them much exhortation, he came into Greece, And there abode three months. And when the Jews laid wait for him, as he was about to sail into Syria, he purposed to return through Macedonia. (Acts 20:1-3)

Philip preached to Gentiles in Samaria. Ethiopian Eunuch was saved. (Ref: Acts Chapter 8). But then there are those who contend that all those in Samaria were of the seed of Jacob. True there were Gentiles from the lineage of Jews in Samaria, but it is too much of an assumption to say that all those in Samaria were the seed of Jacob. The text does not show that proselytes referred to in Acts Chapter 2 were circumcised ones; therefore, it cannot be conclusively said that they were equal to Jews; rather it is apt to say that they were a group of true proselytes and true

Leslie M. John

Gentiles.

God has given enough material in the Scriptures for living a holy life. There were number of incidences shown in the Scriptures and those numbers are enough for us to believe without raising contradictions. Not all the miracles done by Jesus are recorded in the Bible. Similarly not all the acts done by Peter and other disciples or by Apostle Paul were recorded.

## GREAT COMMISSION AFTER ACTS 1:8

Lord Jesus Christ's own words in Matthew 28:18-20, Luke 24:44-49 and John 20:19-23 should be believed as the commission given to all of us to proclaim the Gospel of Jesus Christ to the best of one's capacity in the best possible way irrespective of any signs that may or may not follow the preaching. It is misunderstanding that there is no commission for us to reach out to preach the Gospel of Jesus Christ.

This Great Commission to preach the Gospel of Jesus Christ and that he is the savior of the world was preached by the disciples of Jesus Christ after waiting at Jerusalem and receiving the power of the Holy Spirit. Apostle Paul was not there in Jerusalem when Holy Spirit came upon the disciples of Jesus Christ, but then, he was commissioned by Jesus Christ to go to the Gentiles signifying that all those who are called by God are required to be his witnesses and preach the Gospel of Jesus Christ and proclaim that he is the Savior of the world. Jesus said "I am the way, the truth, and the life; no man cometh unto the Father, but by me". (John 14:6)

## THE GOSPEL OF JESUS CHRIST

"But ye are a chosen generation, a royal priesthood, an holy nation, a peculiar people; that ye should shew forth the praises of him who hath called you out of darkness into his marvellous light" (1 Peter 2:9)

"If any be blameless, the husband of one wife, having faithful children not accused of riot or unruly. For a bishop must be blameless, as the

Leslie M. John

steward of God; not selfwilled, not soon angry, not given to wine, no striker, not given to filthy lucre; But a lover of hospitality, a lover of good men, sober, just, holy, temperate; Holding fast the faithful word as he hath been taught, that he may be able by sound doctrine both to exhort and to convince the gainsayers". (Titus 1:6-9)

While woman may teach the word of God privately at home or in classes/meetings in women's fellowship Bible does not allow them to preach the Gospel of Jesus Christ in public or in Church.

But I suffer not a woman to teach, nor to usurp authority over the man, but to be in silence. (1 Timothy 2:12)

Jesus said:

"And I say also unto thee, That thou art Peter, and upon this rock I will build my church; and the gates of hell shall not prevail against it". (Matthew 16:18)

"Now therefore ye are no more strangers and foreigners, but fellowcitizens with the saints, and of the household of God; And are built upon the foundation of the apostles and prophets, Jesus Christ himself being the chief corner stone" (Ephesians 2:19-20)

"For as the body is one, and hath many members, and all the members of that one body, being many, are one body: so also is Christ. For by one Spirit are we all baptized into one body, whether we be Jews or Gentiles, whether we be bond or free; and have been all made to drink into one Spirit. For the body is not one member, but many" (1 Corinthians 12:12-14)

Apostle Paul was the one who was sent out to preach the Gospel of Jesus Christ to the Gentiles. The salvation is by grace alone through faith in Jesus. Paul said circumcision is not required to be observed. Baptism is not part of salvation. Peter preached baptism as part of salvation but Paul did not preach baptism as part of salvation. There were so much of legalism in Peter's preaching, but in Paul's preaching "Grace" is emphasized upon. This is not to say that they disagreed upon what they

Leslie M. John

agreed upon to preach or preached different Gospels, but Peter basically was preaching in early days only to Jews while Paul preached to Gentiles.

"Then Peter said unto them, Repent, and be baptized every one of you in the name of Jesus Christ for the remission of sins, and ye shall receive the gift of the Holy Ghost". (Acts 2:38)

The only place where Paul's testimony that he baptized is found in Acts 18:8 and he acknowledged it in 1 Corinthians 1:14 "I thank God that I baptized none of you, but Crispus and Gaius"

And Crispus, the chief ruler of the synagogue, believed on the Lord with all his house; and many of the Corinthians hearing believed, and were baptized. (Acts 18:8)

THE COMMISSION TO PREACH THE GOSPEL OF JESUS CHRIST DID NOT END. IT WAS A NEW BEGINING IN ACTS CHAPTER 2 WHEN HOLY SPIRIT WAS POURED OUT AND THE CHURCH CAME INTO EXISTENCE. THE COMFORTER CAME INTO THIS WORLD AS WAS PROMISED AND HE WILL BE GONE AFTER THIS CHURCH AGE CEASES.

"And I will pray the Father, and he shall give you another Comforter, that he may abide with you for ever" (John 14:16)

"All scripture is given by inspiration of God, and is profitable for doctrine, for reproof, for correction, for instruction in righteousness" (2 Timothy 3:16)

Leslie M. John

# CHAPTER 9
# GOD LOVES HIS PEOPLE

"**A**nd I saw thrones, and they sat upon them, and judgment was given unto them: and I saw the souls of them that were beheaded for the witness of Jesus, and for the word of God, and which had not worshipped the beast, neither his image, neither had received his mark upon their foreheads, or in their hands; and they lived and reigned with Christ a thousand years" (Revelation 20:4)

God promised Abraham that in Isaac will be the blessed people who will be His people and He will be their God. Jesus came to save the children of Israel, yet they rejected him. This paved the way for Gentiles to come to him for salvation and secure God's mercy. All those who had believed Jesus as their savior and laid faith in him were saved and likewise all those who believe in him shall be saved. Two thieves were crucified one on either side of Lord Jesus. One of them mocked Jesus while the other sought mercy from Jesus. He prayed that Jesus may remember him when He comes in his Kingdom.

Jesus said to the thief who prayed for mercy that he would be in Paradise the very same day when Jesus died on the cross. Jesus was buried and he rose from the dead on the third day and later ascended into heaven. He is seated on the right hand of the Father in heaven. He will come soon. Salvation is available to anyone who calls upon Jesus for mercy.

Isaiah 40:11 "He shall feed his flock like a shepherd: he shall gather the lambs with his arm, and carry [them] in his bosom, [and] shall gently lead those that are with young".

Israel has become one nation in 1948 but they do not have the shepherd yet. They rejected Jesus as their Messiah and called for his blood to be upon them. Has God forgotten Israel because they rejected him as their Messiah? No. God said "Can a woman forget her sucking child, that she should not have compassion on the son of her womb? yea, they may forget, yet will I not forget thee". Isaiah 49:15.

The things are going to be worse for them that they will call for help from Jesus. He would not come until they realize that they have rejected him and they need him. They will face terrible persecution under Antichrist in the last days. They would cry that the mountains may fall on them and kill them (Rev.6:16). Israel will call upon God during the Great Tribulation period. God is not going to leave them but he will bring them on their knees to call upon his help. Then shall the Lord come to them and be their King of kings and Lord of lords. Jesus will reign for thousand years from the throne of David.

And I will give them an heart to know me, that I am the LORD: and they shall be my people, and I will be their God: for they shall return unto me with their whole heart. (Jeremiah 24:7)
God loved His people but they kept on rejecting him. The consequences, as Paul says, would be:

Tribulation and anguish, upon every soul of man that doeth evil, of the Jew first, and also of the Gentile; (Romans 2:9)

But, all those whose sins are washed in the blood of Jesus, irrespective of Jews or Gentiles will be caught up together to meet the Lord in the air even before the Great Tribulation starts.

"The dead shall rise first and we who are alive and remain shall be caught up together with them in the clouds to meet the Lord in the air: and so shall be ever be with the Lord" (1 Thessalonians 4:16-17)

Apostle Paul writes "For there is no difference between the Jew and the Greek: for the same Lord over all is rich unto all that call upon him". (Romans 10:12)

It is the Church that stands above Jew or Gentile finally and his saints as the bride of Jesus and as the Church that is going to be precious possession of Lord Jesus Christ.

Leslie M. John

## LITTLE LOWER THAN ANGELS

Let us ponder on the creation account mentioned in Genesis Chapter 1. God made heavens, earth, plants, and animals by His word and command, but when it came to make man God took some time to make him in his own image. I was thinking that God may have taken quite a great deal of delight to see tiny flies move around, tiny birds jump around, animals jump around, lions roaring, and elephants moving around. After creating man God desired to have fellowship with him and loved him so much. He gave him a helpmate and the man called her as Woman. The Woman was called as "Eve" because she was the mother of all living. The man was called as "Adam" (Gen. 2:19). The Woman was called as "Eve" (Gen 3:20).

When we create some art-work or draw a picture we are delighted to see our work and appreciate it. We want others to appreciate our work and appreciate us for doing that work. Let us think how much God desires to see we appreciate his work, his wisdom, and his ability to create the universe, the earth, the galaxy, the seas, you and me.

God also created supernatural heavenly beings that are called as Angels. The word in Hebrew and Greek from which the word "Angels" derived was also applied to human messengers. It is recorded in Colossians 1:16 that all things whether visible or invisible were created by God and for him. In Hebrews 1:4-8 it is recorded that the Son of God, Lord Jesus Christ was greater than angels. The Father said "Thou art my Son, this day I have begotten thee" and He has ordered the entire angelic host to worship the Son of God. The Father also said to him that his throne is for and ever and the scepter of righteousness is the scepter of his kingdom.

Yet when Jesus was in the form of man on this earth he was considered as little lower than the angels, just as man was considered as lower than the angels. Man is given the glory and honor to have dominion over all the works of God. The angels are the ministering spirits created by God. He takes care of the children of God. Jesus is always with the saved ones, and many times the children of God see angels helping children of God. Think about the wonderful way God has exalted man.

Leslie M. John

The words of Psalmist as prophesied in Psalm 8:3-9 are repeated in Hebrews 2:6-8 as fulfillment of the prophesy.

"When I consider thy heavens, the work of thy fingers, the moon and the stars, which thou hast ordained; What is man, that thou art mindful of him? and the son of man, that thou visitest him? For thou hast made him a little lower than the angels, and hast crowned him with glory and honour. Thou madest him to have dominion over the works of thy hands; thou hast put all things under his feet: All sheep and oxen, yea, and the beasts of the field" (Psalms 8:3-7)

And, in Hebrews 2:9 we have wonderful declaration that Jesus was made little lower than angels for suffering death on behalf of us and was crowned with glory and honor.

But we see Jesus, who was made a little lower than the angels for the suffering of death, crowned with glory and honour; that he by the grace of God should taste death for every man. (Hebrews 2:9)

Leslie M. John

# EVERYTHING HERE IS DUNG

In the Old Testament the instructions given by God to Abraham to circumcise every male child on the eighth day was a covenant between God and Abraham. (A covenant is a mutual agreement). God said every male child among the seed of Abraham after him, whether he is born in the house, or bought with money of any stranger, one that is not of Abraham's seed shall be circumcised and if anyone was not circumcised that soul shall be cut off from his people. It was equivalent to breaking the covenant.

This covenant was established by God between Him and Abraham that He will be God of Abraham and his posterity through Isaac. God promised Abraham that He will give him the land of Canaan as an everlasting possession. (Genesis 17:7-9)

For a New Testament believer circumcision profits nothing. Apostle Paul emphasized this fact in Romans 2:25 "For circumcision verily profiteth, if thou keep the law: but if thou be a breaker of the law, thy circumcision is made uncircumcision".

Referring to this circumcision, Apostle Paul writes in Philippians 3:4-8 that he was from the stock of Israel, of the tribe of Benjamin, a Pharisee, circumcised on the eighth day. He says that if anyone has more trust in circumcision he would consider himself a better man than any other for having kept the law. He writes that, before he accepted Jesus as his Lord, he had great zeal to persecute the Church. Paul's name was Saul before his conversion to follow Jesus. Perhaps,

Paul would have gained wealth, name and fame if only he continued that which he was doing and in his status as a Pharisee, of the tribe of Benjamin, and with the pride of having been circumcised. But, God's plan was not to let Paul into the world to earn some temporal benefits in this world, but His plan was to use Paul for His glory.

Paul says that he counted all the gain that he had in this world, or that

Leslie M. John

which he would have had in this world by not accepting Jesus as his Savior was of no gain. He says it was all waste and loss. The only thing that counted for him as gain was the excellence of the knowledge of Lord Jesus Christ, whom he called, as 'my Lord'. Paul calls everything of this world is just 'dung', a refuse.

"Yea doubtless, and I count all things but loss for the excellency of the knowledge of Christ Jesus my Lord: for whom I have suffered the loss of all things, and do count them but dung, that I may win Christ" (Philippians 3:8)

## SET AFFECTION ON THINGS ABOVE

Many times when people think that their lives are best fortified the life quickly and easily ends and they leave behind their assets for someone else, not even their close ones, to enjoy. King Solomon enjoyed every kind of blessing and was happy. He acknowledges that God loves a man who is good before Him. He says all the days of a greedy man trying to earn more and more in his life are filled with sorrow, travail and grief with no rest in the night. He says God gives a man who is good in his sight wisdom, knowledge and joy, but to the sinner he gives travail, to gather up and to heap up more. He says it is vanity and vexation of spirit. (Ecclesiastes 2:22-26)

Jesus questions how does it profit man who gains the whole world and loses his own soul? What could a man give in exchange for his soul? To be rich is not sin but fraudulent gain and cheating is sin. Trying to gain riches at the cost of working for God does no good. Matthew 16:26-28 say that Jesus will reward every man according to his works. Apostle Paul also says in 2 Corinthians 5:10 that we shall all stand before the judgment seat of Christ to receive rewards for working for Jesus.

It is indeed hard for a child of God to be in the world and be out of the temptations that this world brings into the lives of a believer. The life in this world for a believer in Christ is not a bed of roses. Satan is always at work. "And no marvel; for Satan himself is transformed into an angel of light". (2 Corinthians 11:14) Unless a believer takes refuge in Christ and

Leslie M. John

encounters Satan in the name of Jesus not even the best and strong believer would win over Satan. Believer has constant struggle against the desires of possession of wealth and not falling into lusts of this world. The wise king Solomon drifted from his good path and married many wives and had concubines. More than his sin of being polygamist having married seven hundred wives, princesses and three hundred concubines he went after other gods namely Ashteroth, the Milcom (1 Kings 11:3 -5). God promised that Solomon's throne will be established for ever and ever but He would chastise Solomon for his iniquity. (2 Samuel 7:13-14)

It so often bothers the mind of believer as how to clothe himself, how will he have food to eat and how his needs would be met with. Jesus asked to take a note of how the lilies of the field grow. He said they neither spin nor do they toil yet Solomon in all his glory was not arrayed like one of them. Jesus asked to have faith that if God can clothe the grass of the field he shall clothe us too (Matthew 6:28-30)

It is, therefore, wise to do some works to gather for ourselves treasures in heaven where neither moth nor rust corrupts our wealth instead of storing up for ourselves treasures upon this earth where moth and rust corrupts and where thieves break through and steal. (Matthew 6:19-20)

Apostle Paul says if we are raised with Christ we should seek the things which are above where Christ sits on the right hand of God and not set our affection on the things on this earth.

"If ye then be risen with Christ, seek those things which are above, where Christ sitteth on the right hand of God. Set your affection on things above, not on things on the earth" (Colossians 3:1-2)

## WE ARE SAFE IN HIS HANDS

Then touched he their eyes, saying, According to your faith be it unto you. (Matthew 9:29)

The blind receive their sight, and the lame walk, the lepers are cleansed, and the deaf hear, the dead are raised up, and the poor have the gospel

Leslie M. John

preached to them. (Matthew 11:5)

 Even though Jesus did miracles, yet Jews, who usually took delight in miracles, did not believe on Him as their Messiah, because they thought their Messiah would come like a king in a royal family. Contrary to their expectations Jesus was born as a poor man in the womb of Virgin Mary conceived of the Holy Ghost.

 After Jesus grew up and started his ministry at the age of about thirty he chose few and called them to be his disciples. One such disciple was Matthew, who was a Publican; he collected customs and tax. Jews hated tax collectors because they were, in collaboration with authorities, harassing them. But then, this tax collector, Matthew, found grace in the sight of the Lord, and he was called to be one of his disciples. Matthew willingly accepted the calling from Jesus and instantly responded by following him.

At one point of time, when Jesus was sitting with tax collectors and sinners, Pharisees, a learned sect of Jews, questioned him as to why he was sitting with them to eat. When Jesus heard that question, he answered and said that those who are healthy do not need a physician, but they that are sick need physician. That was to tell them that the righteous do not need Savior, but sinners do need Savior. Basically, Jesus came for his own people, that is, the Jews; but then the salvation is extended to Gentiles also because Jews rejected Jesus as their "Messiah".

The miracles that Jesus would do were prophesied in Isaiah 35:5-6 "Then the eyes of the blind shall be opened, and the ears of the deaf shall be unstopped. Then shall the lame man leap as an hart, and the tongue of the dumb sing: for in the wilderness shall waters break out, and streams in the desert". The prophecy was fulfilled when Jesus healed the sick. God said to the children of Israel through Moses that if they "hearkened diligently to the LORD", the Lord would not bring upon them any of the diseases that He brought upon Egyptians (Exodus 15:26). But they disobeyed God several times and their disobedience needed reconciliation. Adam rebelled against God by transgressing the commandment of God. Bible records that we are all sinners by birth and there is no one righteous.

Leslie M. John

According to 1 John 1:8 "If we say that we have no sin, we deceive ourselves, and the truth is not in us". The Children of Israel transgressed the commandments of God several times.

In order to reconcile man with God, the Son of God, Jesus came into this world in the form of man to take upon our sins on him and die in our place that whosoever believes on him shall receive salvation and be saved from eternal damnation. God loved man so much that He gave his one and only Son, Jesus Christ that whoever believes in him shall be saved.

Friend, are you burdened with the thought that your sin is too great that it cannot be forgiven? Please be sure that every sin, except blasphemy of the Holy Spirit, is pardonable by God.
"Come unto me, all ye that labour and are heavy laden, and I will give you rest" (Matthew 11:28)

## PUT ON THE ARMOUR OF GOD

"Put on the whole armour of God, that ye may be able to stand against the wiles of the devil". (Ephesians 6:11)
In the battle that was to take place between the army of Philistines and the army of children of Israel both were advantageously posted, yet neither went forward to fight against each other. Philistine hero Goliath was waiting for an equivalent opponent. Saul thought there was none on his side to fight against this mighty proud warrior.

David the youngest son of Jesse, looking after his father's sheep, went to watch as to what was happening in the battlefield. To his surprise, he found that none from the Israelites' camp went forward to fight against Goliath. Deeply distressed over the attitude of his brothers and also that of others in the camp, he agreed to fight with Goliath. He retorted saying, "Who is this uncircumcised fellow to mock at God's children?" David took the challenge and went forward to face Goliath.

Seeing the shepherd boy the giant Goliath insulted him. David was a shepherd boy, short in stature and did not attire himself in good dress.

Leslie M. John

Saul was worried about the intervention of this shepherd boy, David. "And Saul said to David, Thou art not able to go against this Philistine to fight with him: for thou art but a youth, and he a man of war from his youth". (1 Samuel 17:33) What a discouragement David had to face from Saul!

Yet after hearing David's courageous acts Saul conceded to David to fight against the Philistine but asked David to wear "his armour, and he put on helmet of brass upon his head and also armed him with a coat of mail". (1 Samuel 17:38).

Saul thought armor, helmet of brass and coat are required to meet challenge of enemy. He insisted upon David to wear armor of his choice to face Goliath. Saul himself did not have courage to face Goliath but he thought David needed his choice armor to face the enemy. David girded his sword upon his armour and found uncomfortable. He removed it saying that he can not go with the armour that Saul has provided him. (1 Samuel 17:39)

David took his staff and chose five smooth stones out of the brook and he slang a stone from his sling. The stone sunk into Goliath's forehead and he fell upon his face to the earth. (1 Samuel 17:40 and 49)

David ran and stood upon Philistine and took his sword and killed him and the philistines fled from the battlefield (1 Samuel 17:50-51)

David used Goliath's own weapon to kill him. God was with David. Goliath's strength and power were of no avail before God's.

The same God, the living Lord, who has sent His Son, Jesus Christ, into this world for the remission of your sins and mine, calls us to depend on Him because He is our savior. He wants to be our rock of refuge and bless us. He wants us to put on the armour that he gave us instead of putting on the armour that the world gives us. Let not the strong man glory in his strength.

Leslie M. John

# CHAPTER 10
# THE CHURCH
# THE BODY OF CHRIST

We would know the true meaning of the Church if we could appreciate the words of Adam when he saw the woman. The LORD God caused a deep sleep to fall upon Adam and when he was sleeping God took one of his ribs and closed up the flesh in its place. God made the rib of man a woman and brought the woman unto man.

"And Adam said, This is now bone of my bones, and flesh of my flesh: she shall be called Woman, because she was taken out of Man". (Genesis 2:23)
The word of God says:

"Therefore shall a man leave his father and his mother, and shall cleave unto his wife: and they shall be one flesh". (Genesis 2:24)

This glorious truth is presented to us by Apostle Paul in Ephesians 5:22-25

"Wives, submit yourselves unto your own husbands, as unto the Lord. For the husband is the head of the wife, even as Christ is the head of the church: and he is the saviour of the body. Therefore as the church is subject unto Christ, so let the wives be to their own husbands in everything. Husbands, love your wives, even as Christ also loved the church, and gave himself for it" (Ephesians 5:22-25)

The relationship between the husband and the wife is that husband is the head of the wife, even as Christ is the head of the Church. Christ is the savior of the body and he presents to himself a bride that is holy and without blemish.

Page 115

Leslie M. John

"That he might present it to himself a glorious church, not having spot, or wrinkle, or any such thing; but that it should be holy and without blemish". (Ephesians 5:27)

All those whose sin is cleansed by the blood of Christ are the members of the Church, which is the body of Christ.

"Now ye are the body of Christ, and members in particular". (1 Corinthians 12:27)

The body of Christ is one and has many members who are the members of that one body, and being many members they are all one body. The body of Christ is baptized by one Spirit irrespective of whether we are Jews or Gentiles, or bond or free. One part of the body cannot say to the other that it has no need of the other. Foot cannot call itself separate from the body because it is not hand, nor can eye can call itself separate because it is not ear, nor can anybody part say to the other that it has no need of the other part (1 Corinthians 12:12-24). The whole body suffers if one of its members suffers loss or damage.

Church is not a building or simply a called out people, or congregation, or gathering of citizens, or social gathering, or discussion or debating forum. It is not also the "kingdom of heaven" or "kingdom of God". The Church is the "Body of Christ". The Church is the "Bride of Christ". Careful observation of Ephesians Chapter 5 gives us the answer that the one who is presenting to Himself is Lord Jesus Christ and He is presenting to Himself a glorious Church that has no spot, or wrinkle of any such thing. Jesus is expecting from the Church that it should be without blemish.

What is the purpose of Jesus presenting to himself Church without blemish? It is because the Church is His bride, His own possession which was bought with a price and that price was His own blood shed on the cross. Christ is the head of the Church and He is the savior of the body. The Church is subject unto Jesus Christ, who loved it so much so that he says a husband should love his wife just as He loved the Church. (Ephesians 5:23-25)

Leslie M. John

We also derive knowledge about "Church" from referring to Lexicon Hebrew Strong's Number 6951 and Greek Strong's Number 1577.

Hebrew Strong's Number: 6951 is "lhq" transliterated as "Qahal" pronounced as " kaw-hawl'" Its definition is: assembly, company, congregation, convocation, assembly for evil counsel, war or invasion, religious purposes, company (of returning exiles), congregation as organized body. The word occurs in the Old Testament 123 times in KJV – 17 times as "assembly" 17 times as "company" 86 times as "congregation" and 3 times as "multitude".

Greek Strong's Number: 1577 is: "eÍkklhsiða" transliterated as: "Ekklesia" pronounced as "ek-klay-see'-ah". Its definition is: "gathering of citizens called out from their homes into some public place", or "an assembly" or "an assembly of the people convened at the public place of the council for the purpose of deliberating" It could be "the assembly of the Israelites", "any gathering or throng of men assembled by chance, tumultuously" and in Christian sense "an assembly of Christians gathered for worship in a religious meeting". The word occurs in New Testament 118 times in KJV; 3 times as "Assembly" and 115 times as "Church".

The following few verses also help us to understand the meaning of the Church.

"And I say also unto thee, That thou art Peter, and upon this rock I will build my church; and the gates of hell shall not prevail against it". (Matthew 16:18)

"Praising God, and having favour with all the people. And the Lord added to the church daily such as should be saved". (Acts 2:47)

At the coasts of Caesarea Philippi Jesus asked his disciples as to what men say that He was? The disciples said some say that Jesus was John the Baptist, and some say that He was Prophet Elijah, and others Prophet Jeremiah or one of the prophets. But then, Jesus emphatically asked his disciples as to what they say of him. Simon Peter, quick as he was always, said that Jesus was the Christ that is He was the Messiah, and the Jesus

Leslie M. John

was the Son of the living God. What a great testimony Peter gave of Jesus! Then Jesus blessed Peter and said that flesh and blood did not reveal that fact to him but the Father in heaven. Jesus continued blessing him and said that Peter was the rock that He would build His Church and gates of hell shall not prevail against the Church that Jesus builds on him.

There is no question of doubting here that Jesus was saying simply that he was going to build the Church on that rock nearby but Peter was the rock on whom Jesus was going to build the Church. Jesus was pointing to a future event and, therefore, there is no reason to believe that the Church had already begun. There are few points that are very clear here. That Jesus was going to build the Church; that Jesus was going to build the Church on Peter; that the Church did not begin until then.

Holy Spirit came upon all those who were waiting at Jerusalem as instructed by Lord Jesus Christ and they were all filled with Holy Spirit and began to speak with other tongues as the Spirit gave them utterance. There were Jews, devout men, out of every nation under heaven at Jerusalem on that day (Acts 2:4, 5). Some mocked saying that they were drunk, but Peter said that they were not drunk but that was what was spoken of prophet Joel spoke that God will pour out His "Spirit upon all flesh: and your sons and your daughters shall prophesy, and your young men shall see visions, and your old men shall dream dreams" (Acts 2:16-17, Joel 2:28).

Peter was the first disciple who spoke of Lord Jesus Christ's death on the cross, his burial and resurrection. Many from the audience received the word and "Then they that gladly received his word were baptized: and the same day there were added unto them about three thousand souls" (Acts 2:41).

As we read Acts Chapter 2 further we see that the Lord added to the church daily such as should be saved. It is clear here that the Church came into existence on Pentecost day as we read in Acts Chapter 2 and three thousand souls were added to the church and then the Lord added to the Church daily such as should be saved. (Acts 2:47)

Leslie M. John

Acts Chapter 11:1 says that apostles and brethren who were in Judea heard that Gentiles had also received the word of God. When Peter went to Jerusalem they questioned him as to why he ate with those who were un-circumcised. Peter told them entire happening about how Cornelius, an un-circumcised Gentile was saved and how God told them not to treat anything as unclean (Acts Chapters 9 and 10). This record shows that Gentiles were added to the Church. Neither Bible nor secular history says that all those who are from the regions mentioned in Acts 2 were pure descendants of Jacob. The commission, indeed, was first to preach in Jerusalem, then in Judea and Samaria, and then to the uttermost part of the earth; but we see here that Gentiles heard the Gospel and were saved. They became part of the Church. They were called "Christians" first at Antioch.

Saul was converted and was named Paul and then in due course of time Barnabas departed to Tarsus to seek Saul. When he found him he brought him to Antioch and they assembled with the church and taught much people. They were then called "Christians" first at Antioch.

"Then departed Barnabas to Tarsus, for to seek Saul: And when he had found him, he brought him unto Antioch. And it came to pass, that a whole year they assembled themselves with the church, and taught much people. And the disciples were called Christians first in Antioch". (Acts 11:25-26)

The Church/Ekklesia that Lord Jesus Christ intended it to be like are not

1. A gathering of citizens called out from their homes into some public place.
2. The whole body of nominal Christians scattered throughout the earth etc.

There is a tendency to link of the word Hebrew Word "qahal" of the Old Testament with the Greek word "ekklesia" in the New Testament based on the relationship that is present in Hebrews 2:12 with that of Psalm 22:22 and Matthew 26:30 and interpret that the Church was already begun in Matthew 26:30 with Jesus singing song along with his disciples

Leslie M. John

after the Lord's Supper was instituted by Jesus Christ.

While this relationship is true and also that Jesus and disciples sang a song after the Passover is true these were only the basic elements shown in the case of Church/ekklesia. God never intended to build Church/ekklesia with only Jews and/or his disciples. That is not the right way of dividing the Scriptures.

"Study to shew thyself approved unto God, a workman that needeth not to be ashamed, rightly dividing the word of truth" (2 Timothy 2:15)

"And I say also unto thee, That thou art Peter, and upon this rock I will build my church; and the gates of hell shall not prevail against it". (Matthew 16:18)

The crucifixion of Jesus was yet to come when he instituted the Lord's Supper. Secondly, Matthew 28:18-19 Commission did not come into effect until after Pentecost was fully come and Holy Spirit came upon all those who were waiting at Jerusalem as per the instruction of Jesus. The commission came into effect only after Acts 1:8

"But ye shall receive power, after that the Holy Ghost is come upon you: and ye shall be witnesses unto me both in Jerusalem, and in all Judaea, and in Samaria, and unto the uttermost part of the earth" (Acts 1:8)

"And there were dwelling at Jerusalem Jews, devout men, out of every nation under heaven. Now when this was noised abroad, the multitude came together, and were confounded, because that every man heard them speak in his own language. And they were all amazed and marvelled, saying one to another, Behold, are not all these which speak Galilaeans? And how hear we every man in our own tongue, wherein we were born? Parthians, and Medes, and Elamites, and the dwellers in Mesopotamia, and in Judaea, and Cappadocia, in Pontus, and Asia, Phrygia, and Pamphylia, in Egypt, and in the parts of Libya about Cyrene, and strangers of Rome, Jews and proselytes, Cretes and Arabians, we do hear them speak in our tongues the wonderful works of God". (Acts 2:5-11)

Leslie M. John

There is a long list of countries, cities, towns mentioned in Acts 2:5-11. There is considerable disagreement about the people from these regions who were at Jerusalem during Passover festival, Unleavened bread and First-fruits, and Pentecost. The disagreement is as to whether they were Jews only or Jews and others. Except for feast of Pentecost all other feasts had just been over at the time when Jesus gave instructions to his disciples to wait at Jerusalem until they receive power from heaven to go to nations to proclaim the Gospel of Jesus Christ.

Apostles had not yet preached the Gospel of Jesus Christ until then. Prior to ascension of Jesus Christ into heaven all that they knew was about probable restoration of the kingdom. They asked Jesus when He would restore the kingdom; but He gave them reply that it was not for them to know the time that was in the authority of His Father (Acts 1:7). That was a feast time and when people gathered at Jerusalem to celebrate the festival and many others, who were, perhaps at there to do business.

There is no indication that all that were at Jerusalem at that time were Jews only. It reads "Jews, devout men, out of every nation under heaven". If only Jews were there then other names would not have been there, but presence of other names and other regions confirms that the people there were not only Jews but Gentiles also. Scriptures and secular history do not say that "Parthians", "Medes", and "Elamites" were Jews. Genesis Chapter 10 and genuine historical record of Flavius Joseph proves that those present at Jerusalem during the feast of Pentecost were descendants of Jacob and also Gentiles.

Jesus said he will build the Church on Peter whom He compared with the rock (Petra) and said that the gates of hell shall not prevail against the Church (Matthew 16:18). Peter spoke and testified the death, burial and resurrection of Jesus Christ. Acts 2:14-33. This is the first ever proclamation of the death of Jesus, his burial and resurrection was made and it was done by the one whom Jesus spoke of earlier. When Peter spoke of Jesus Christ there were three thousands souls added to them. It is very apt to note here that the audience present when Peter spoke about Jesus Christ was not only Jews but many others. Peter addressed

Leslie M. John

them as "Men and brethren".

"Men and brethren, this scripture must needs have been fulfilled, which the Holy Ghost by the mouth of David spake before concerning Judas, which was guide to them that took Jesus" (Acts 1:16)

It should be noted that there were not only Jews but many others were present at the time when Peter spoke. It cannot be said that they were all the direct descendants of Jacob to believe that only Jews were there at that time. This alleviates the thought that there were no Gentiles when Peter spoke. Surely there were Gentiles. This is the first time Peter spoke about the Jesus Christ's death, burial and resurrection and this is the first time that there were three thousand souls were added to them.

According to the commission given by Lord Jesus Christ the disciples were asked to be his witnesses first in Jerusalem, and in all Judea and in Samaria, and then in the uttermost part of the earth (Acts 1:8).

Basically it means that the message of salvation should have been spoken to first to Jews, then to descendants of Jews who mixed with Gentiles, and then lastly to the Gentiles. Peter and other disciples surely followed just as Lord Jesus Christ commanded. However, it is too much to presume that there were no Gentiles in Jerusalem when Peter was speaking to Jews. If only Jews were present and none else, then it would also mean that only Jews crucified Jesus and no Gentile was responsible for crucifixion of Jesus. Obviously it means Gentiles would never be partakers of the death, burial and resurrection of Jesus. This is not the case.

Those, who crucified Jesus, were representatives of you and me. It is our sin that crucified Jesus. It is because of all of us that Jesus died on the cross taking on himself our sin to redeem us from the bondage of sin.

"For he hath made him to be sin for us, who knew no sin; that we might be made the righteousness of God in him" (2 Corinthians 5:21)

It is hard to find evidence in the Scriptures or in the secular history if the people in the regions mentioned in Acts 2:9-10 or in 1 Peter 1:1 are the

Leslie M. John

descendants of Jacob. If no evidence can be produced then there is no meaning in saying that a distinct dispensation started after Acts Chapter 28 as "One New Man". The Church consists of Jews and Gentiles and the Church came into existence as recorded in Acts Chapter 2. All those who are saved by grace through faith in Jesus are the members of the Church and the Church is the "Body of Christ" Jesus is the head of the Church. The Church is bought with the price and that price is the blood of Lord Jesus. No doubt, Jews were there at the time of crucifixion of Jesus and also on the day of Pentecost, but it is too much to say that there were ONLY JEWS! Scriptures should speak of Scriptures and confirm them and not mere assumptions. How sure is anyone to say that none of the Gentiles, not even Roman Soldiers, or Government Officials, were saved when Peter preached about Jesus in Acts 2? It is mere speculation that only Jews were saved when Peter preached.

The Church grew and the Lord added to the Church souls daily as such as should be saved (Acts 2:47). The Scriptures call this collection of believers who are the members of His body and worship him as the "Church". Furthermore the members of this Church, who taught the word of God to much people became the disciples of Jesus and these disciples were called first in Antioch (Acts 11:26). The commission of Jesus was to teach and make disciples of all nations, baptizing them in the name of the Father, and of the Son, and of the Holy Spirit. (Matthew 28:18-20)

Peter surely was addressing Jews in Acts 3:25-26 that they are the children of prophets, and of the covenant and that their fathers were Abraham, Isaac, and Jacob, unto whose children were the foremost privileges given of turning away from their iniquities and repent believing that God raised up his Son Jesus from the dead. They were surely blessed ones. It is by grace by faith in Jesus that we are all saved. The children of Jacob refused to accept Jesus as their Messiah and then the disciples turned to Gentiles. There is not much record of his disciples preaching to the Gentiles. God kept their itineraries and preaching and where the lost ten tribes were as mystery to us. However, Paul's itineraries are recorded. Paul also preached first to Jews and then turned to Gentiles.

Leslie M. John

In Acts 13:46-47 we see that Paul and Barnabas became bold and said that it was necessary for them that the word of God should have been preached to Jews first. When they rejected their preaching they turned to Gentiles. Paul claims that he was chosen to be the light of the Gentiles and that he should speak of salvation unto the ends of the earth. (Acts 13:46-47)

The Lord spoke to Ananias about Paul that he was chosen vessel unto Him to bear His name before the Gentiles, and kings and the children of Israel.

"But the Lord said unto him, Go thy way: for he is a chosen vessel unto me, to bear my name before the Gentiles, and kings, and the children of Israel": (Acts 9:15)

Later on Paul became a very strong witness of Lord Jesus Christ and in spite of facing many trials and tribulations even imprisonment he did not give up preaching the Gospel of Jesus Christ. Paul said he was not ashamed of the gospel of Christ, because it was the power of God unto salvation first to Jew and then to Gentiles.

"For I am not ashamed of the gospel of Christ: for it is the power of God unto salvation to everyone that believeth; to the Jew first, and also to the Greek". (Romans 1:16)
For some people these verses may appear to be unimportant, but these verses surely help to form a solid ground for preaching Gospel (Cf. Acts Chapter 2:9-11 – They were all not Jews!)

I Chronicles Chapter 1:

Vs. 17 The sons of Shem; Elam, and Asshur, and Arphaxad, and Lud, and Aram, and Uz, and Hul, and Gether, and Meshech.
Vs 18 And Arphaxad begat Shelah, and Shelah begat Eber.
Vs 19 And unto Eber were born two sons: the name of the one was Peleg; because in his days the earth was divided: and his brother's name was Joktan.

Leslie M. John

Vs 20 And Joktan begat Almodad, and Sheleph, and Hazarmaveth, and Jerah,

Vs 21 Hadoram also, and Uzal, and Diklah,

Vs 22 And Ebal, and Abimael, and Sheba,

Vs 23 And Ophir, and Havilah, and Jobab. All these were the sons of Joktan. Vs 24 Shem, Arphaxad, Shelah,

Vs 25 Eber, Peleg, Reu,

Vs 26 Serug, Nahor, Terah,

Vs 27 Abram; the same is Abraham.

Vs 28 The sons of Abraham; Isaac, and Ishmael.

Josephus, the noted historian says:
"the sons of Japhet; from Madai came the Madeans, who are called Medes, by the Greeks;"

"So did Riphath found the Ripheans, now called Paphlagonians; and Thrugramma the Thrugrammeans, who, as the Greeks resolved, were named Phrygians"
... and yet some Christians say that the three thousand souls saved (Acts 2:41) were all Jews!

The following is an excerpt from Flavius Joseph's record:

Quote: 4. Shem, the third son of Noah, had five sons, who inhabited the land that began at Euphrates, and reached to the Indian Ocean. For Elam left behind him the Elamites, the ancestors of the Persians. Ashur lived at the city Nineve; and named his subjects Assyrians, who became the most fortunate nation, beyond others. Arphaxad named the Arphaxadites, who are now called Chaldeans. Aram had the Aramites, which the Greeks called Syrians; as Laud founded the Laudites, which are now called Lydians. Of the four sons of Aram, Uz founded Trachonitis and Damascus: this country lies between Palestine and Celesyria. Ul founded Armenia; and Gather the Bactrians; and Mesa the Mesaneans; it is now called Charax Spasini. Sala was the son of Arphaxad; and his son was Heber, from whom they originally called the Jews Hebrews. Heber begat Joetan and Phaleg: he was called Phaleg, because he was born at the dispersion of the nations to their several countries; for Phaleg among the

Hebrews signifies division. Now Joctan, one of the sons of Heber, had these sons, Elmodad, Saleph, Asermoth, Jera, Adoram, Aizel, Decla, Ebal, Abimael, Sabeus, Ophir, Euilat, and Jobab. These inhabited from Cophen, an Indian river, and in part of Asia adjoining to it. And this shall suffice concerning the sons of Shem.

5. I will now treat of the Hebrews. The son of Phaleg, whose father was Heber, was Ragau; whose son was Serug, to whom was born Nahor; his son was Terah, who was the father of Abraham, who accordingly was the tenth from Noah, and was born in the two hundred and ninety-second year after the deluge; for Terah begat Abram in his seventieth year. Nahor begat Haran when he was one hundred and twenty years old; Nahor was born to Serug in his hundred and thirty-second year; Ragau had Serug at one hundred and thirty; at the same age also Phaleg had Ragau; Heber begat Phaleg in his hundred and thirty-fourth year; he himself being begotten by Sala when he was a hundred and thirty years old, whom Arphaxad had for his son at the hundred and thirty-fifth year of his age. Arphaxad was the son of Shem, and born twelve years after the deluge. Now Abram had two brethren, Nahor and Haran: of these Haran left a son, Lot; as also Sarai and Milcha his daughters; and died among the Chaldeans, in a city of the Chaldeans, called Ur; and his monument is shown to this day. These married their nieces. Nabor married Milcha, and Abram married Sarai. Now Terah hating Chaldea, on account of his mourning for Ilaran, they all removed to Haran of Mesopotamia, where Terah died, and was buried, when he had lived to be two hundred and five years old; Unquote

## THE BIRTH OF THE CHURCH

In Acts 1:4 we read that the disciples of Jesus were commanded not to depart from Jerusalem but wait for the Promise of the Father (Luke 24:49)

"And, being assembled together with [them], commanded them that they should not depart from Jerusalem, but wait for the promise of the Father, which, [saith he], ye have heard of me"

Leslie M. John

"And suddenly there came a sound from heaven as of a rushing mighty wind, and it filled all the house where they were sitting. And there appeared unto them cloven tongues like as of fire, and it sat upon each of them". (Acts 2:2-3)

After the ascension of Jesus they returned unto Jerusalem and they went up into upper room and they all continued in prayer with one accord. As we see in Acts Chapter 1:13 the disciples of Jesus, with the women, and Mary the mother of Jesus and with his brethren were in upper room and continued with one accord in prayer and supplication.

Acts 1:13 "And when they were come in, they went up into an upper room, where abode both Peter, and James, and John, and Andrew, Philip, and Thomas, Bartholomew, and Matthew, James [the son] of Alphaeus, and Simon Zelotes, and Judas [the brother] of James."

The narration continues to verse 15 which says that in those days Peter stood up in the midst of all of them who were one hundred and twenty in number and spoke to them.

In Acts Chapter 2 we see that the day of Pentecost had finally come and they were all with one accord in one place. The sequence of the important three feasts was the Passover, the first-fruits and the Pentecost. Detailed description of all the feasts is listed in Leviticus Chapter 23. On the day of Passover Jesus was crucified; on the day of first-fruits Jesus rose from the dead and on the day of Pentecost the Church was born.

Jesus is called the firstfruits as we read in 1 Corinthians 15:23 "But every man in his own order: Christ the firstfruits; afterward they that are Christ's at his coming".

After Jesus rose from the dead he asked his disciples to wait at Jerusalem to receive the power. Jesus said to them they will be his witnesses after they receive the promise of the Father and that power was the Holy Spirit. The promise of the Father that is the Holy Spirit came upon all the one hundred and twenty people including the disciples of Jesus and the

Leslie M. John

mother of Jesus. It was fiftieth day after the Passover feast. It was on Pentecost when the Holy Spirit came from heaven upon all those who were in upper room where the Church came into existence. We are not asked to wait to receive the Holy Spirit, but He takes residence in every believer at the time of accepting Jesus as Savior.

There came from heaven, not from anywhere else, a sound from heaven as of a rushing mighty wind. The sound was from heaven and it was like a rushing mighty wind. It was not wind but it was like a rushing wind and when that sound came from heaven it filled the entire house where they were sitting. Then there appeared unto them cloven tongues like of fire, not fire, but it was like fire and it sat upon each of them. There was no exclusion, but all of them had the cloven tongues like fire, not exactly fire, upon them. "Cloven" is past participle of "cleave". That means everyone in the upper room saw the split or divided tongues like that of fire that came upon and sitting upon each of them. When they were waiting in the upper room as Jesus commanded them to do, suddenly there came a sound from heaven like that of a rushing mighty wind, and it filled the entire house where they were sitting. Then there appeared to them split tongues like as of fire, not exactly fire, and it sat upon each one of them.

The promise of the Father was that they will not be left like orphans but the Comforter that is The Holy Spirit will be with them always. When they received the Holy Spirit they began to speak with other tongues as the Spirit gave them utterance. They spoke in other tongues as the Spirit gave them utterance. They spoke different languages. Their speaking was not the utterance from the choices that the individuals could make, but it was as the Spirit gave them the utterance.

John said: "John answered them, saying, I baptize with water: but there standeth one among you, whom ye know not". John 1:26
Mar 1:8 I indeed have baptized you with water: but he shall baptize you with the Holy Ghost.

In Acts Chapter 2 what we see is that disciples were gathered in

Leslie M. John

obedience to the commandment of Jesus. The occasion was the day of the birth of the Church; that is fiftieth day after the Passover feast and it was during the feast days in Jerusalem. The utterances were the languages of the earth which every one of them understood. It was the time of three important feasts. Firstly, it was of Passover, secondly it was of first-fruits, and thirdly it was of Pentecost. There were Jews, devout men, out of every nation under heaven in Jerusalem. When they all in Jerusalem heard the sound of the noise that came down from heaven like that of a mighty wind they were all surprised. There was no mighty wind but they heard the sound of the mighty wind that came down from heaven.

There was multitude of people in Jerusalem. There were Parthians, and Medes, and Elamites, and the dwellers in Mesopotamia, and in Judaea, and Cappadocia, in Pontus, and Asia, Phrygia, and Pamphylia, in Egypt, and in the parts of Libya about Cyrene, and strangers of Rome, Jews and proselytes, Cretes and Arabians. The text in Acts 2:5-13 does not show that these all men were circumcised Proselytes. They all understood the languages that they spoke to one another and they marveled to see the signs and wonders of God. They were all amazed and some mocked saying that they were drunk, but Peter lifted up his voice and said to them that they were not drunk. Peter said that as spoken by the Prophet Joel they all spoke in languages which were understood by all of them. (Acts 2:1-20)

## SEQUENCE OF PROCLAMATION OF GOSPEL

"And, being assembled together with them, commanded them that they should not depart from Jerusalem, but wait for the promise of the Father, which, saith he, ye have heard of me" (Acts 1:4)

There was an order and sequence by which the Gospel of Jesus Christ was to be proclaimed since the ascension of Jesus Christ into heaven. This sequence was given by Jesus Christ himself. Even though the disciples were curious to know certain things even before those things were supposed to be known, Jesus commanded them to follow the

Leslie M. John

sequence.

Firstly, they were asked not to be concerned of the time when the kingdom shall be restored to Israel. Secondly, they were asked to wait at Jerusalem to receive the promise of the Father and that promise was the coming of the Holy Spirit upon them. Jesus promised to the disciples that they would not be left as orphans but The Comforter will be with them always. Thirdly, they were asked to go to one region first and then to another region and so on and after giving them the order, Jesus ascended into heaven. The disciples did just as Jesus told them to do. They waited at Jerusalem and received the Holy Spirit and power came upon them. The Holy Spirit is right here as The Comforter.

The book of Acts is a systematic and detailed exposition written by Luke who wrote the Gospel of Luke. In continuation of all that Jesus taught until he ascended Luke also wrote about the infallible proofs Jesus left behind during the period of forty days between his resurrection from the dead and ascension into heaven.

Before ascension Jesus spoke to his disciples about the kingdom. The disciples were curious to know when he would restore the kingdom to Israel. Jesus told them that it is not for them to know the times and seasons that the Father had put in his own power. He said to them that they would receive the power after the Holy Spirit comes upon them. Then, they would be his witnesses both in Jerusalem and in all Judea and in Samaria and then in uttermost parts of the earth. One noticeable fact here is the sequence that was to be followed for proclamation of the Gospel of Jesus Christ. First it would be in Jerusalem, his own place and to his own people, second it would be in Judea and Samaria, where Israelites and Gentiles lived, and lastly it would be to the utmost part of the earth; that is to everyone. These three stages are seen in Acts from Chapters 1-7, second from Chapters 8 to 12 and third from Chapters 13 to 28.

After Jesus spoke about these things to his disciples a cloud received Jesus as he ascended into heaven and they saw him no more. While the disciples looked steadfastly and watched two men stood by them in

Leslie M. John

white apparel and said that Jesus who ascended into heaven will come back in the same way as he ascended.

Then they return to Mount of Olives which is at a distance of one Sabbath day's journey. (Sabbath day's journey is equivalent to seven and half furlongs and not a mile; this distance was based on conventional agreement among Jews as the distance that they can walk on a Sabbath day). The disciples and others that were in upper room were one hundred and twenty in number Peter took leadership and spoke to them (Acts 1:6-15). Mathias was numbered along with eleven disciples by lots to replace Judas Iscariot, who betrayed Jesus.

In the early days of proclamation of Gospel of Jesus Christ by the Apostles the power of God was seen clearly.

# CHAPPTER 11
# KINGDOM OF HEAVEN AND
# KINGDOM OF GOD

I have dealt with seven points here.

1.The phrases "Kingdom of Heaven" and "Kingdom of God" are interchangeably used in the four Gospels while dealing with parallel themes.

2.Jesus is indeed the King of the Jews.

3.Jesus is not called the "King of the Church" but is called as "Head of the Church"

4.The Church came into existence as recorded in Acts Chapter 2 and not after the Acts 28 period.

5.The earthly mission of Jesus was for restoration of kingdom to Jews, but then because Jews rejected him as "Messiah" the salvation is extended to Gentiles as well.

6.The literal "Kingdom of Heaven" will come into existence when Lord Jesus Christ rules from the throne of David during the thousand-year-reign.

7.The "Kingdom of God" not only includes the millennial rule of Lord Jesus Christ but it has several aspects as we read in the parables mentioned in Matthew Chapter 13

"Be it known therefore unto you, that the salvation of God is sent unto the Gentiles, and that they will hear it" (Acts 28:28).

"Preaching the kingdom of God, and teaching those things which concern the Lord Jesus Christ, with all confidence, no man forbidding

Leslie M. John

him". (Acts 28:31)

Going by the text from verse 23 to 31 of Acts Chapter 28 it is evident that Jews rejected the message from Apostle Paul. The message he expounded there was about the kingdom of God, both out of the Law of Moses, and out of the prophets from morning till evening and yet only some believed and some did not believe. The phrases "kingdom of heaven" and "kingdom of God" were interchangeably used in the four Gospels. In the Gospel of Matthew the phrase used was "kingdom of heaven" and it appears in other Gospels as "kingdom of God". Some have interpreted differentiating this phrase as different from one another.

Jesus indeed came in search of the lost sheep of Israel:

"These twelve Jesus sent forth, and commanded them, saying, Go not into the way of the Gentiles, and into any city of the Samaritans enter ye not: But go rather to the lost sheep of the house of Israel. And as ye go, preach, saying, The kingdom of heaven is at hand." (Matthew 10:5-7)

While it is true that Lord Jesus Christ sets up literal rule for thousand years on this earth at his second advent, the phrase used in four Gospels speak of the same kingdom although the Matthew preferred to call it as "kingdom of heaven". The message Paul spoke on different occasions before he finally settled to speak to the Gentiles was about Salvation which is free gift and is not associated with law and works. The message Peter spoke initially was about the "kingdom of God" to Jews before he spoke to Gentiles.

The Kingdom, which was originally supposed to come into existence, provided Jews accepted Jesus as their Messiah was postponed to accommodate Gentiles in the Church. Jews rejected Jesus as their Messiah and this eventually paved the way for Gentiles to come into the Church. But then, was this a happening without the knowledge of God? No, God had salvation to Gentiles in his plan and deliberately blinded the eyes of Jews. (Romans Chapters.9-11)

Jesus is not referred to as "King of the Church" but He is called "Head of

Leslie M. John

the Church" and all the believers saved are His body and they are called the "Body of Christ". The title of Jesus as "Christ" means that He is the Savior and He is the "Messiah" about whom the prophets prophesied. About Jesus was written in the books of Moses. The first one from Gentile to be saved was Cornelius, who was uncircumcised Gentile. The scriptures do not show anywhere that he was circumcised or grafted to become proselyte or have the privileges of Jews. Paul says in his epistles that Jews and Gentiles in the Body of Christ have equal privileges. It was this mystery hidden in God the Gentiles should be partakers and become fellow heirs of Jews (Ephesians 3:2 and 3:6). This mystery was hidden in God even from the foundations of the earth.

Magi recognized Jesus as the King of the Jews. It is worth noticing that the wise men from the east came to Jerusalem to see the child Jesus and even before they saw him they recognized him as the King of the Jews born in Bethlehem. King Herod was also troubled. He inquired of the child and when wise men did not go back to him to give information that he needed he was filled with anger and slew all the children of the age up to two in Bethlehem, but by then Jesus was taken to Egypt by his parents. The wise men worshipped neither the mother of Jesus nor Joseph, but worshipped the child Jesus in Bethlehem.

"Saying, Where is he that is born King of the Jews? for we have seen his star in the east, and are come to worship him". (Matthew 2:2)

Jesus accepted worship as the King of Jews: In Matthew Chapter 21:1-11 there is a description as to how Jesus sent two disciples to get a donkey and a colt with her. He said to them that if anyone asked them as to what they were doing he said that they should say to them that the Lord needs them. The disciples did as were commanded by Jesus. Great multitude spread their garments in the way and some others sprayed branches of trees while Jesus rode on that donkey. The multitudes that went before and that followed him cried saying: "Hosanna to the Son of David: Blessed is he that cometh in the name of the Lord; Hosanna in the highest"

"Tell ye the daughter of Sino, Behold, thy King cometh unto thee, meek,

Leslie M. John

and sitting upon an ass, and a colt the foal of an ass". (Matthew 21:5)

"Behold, the LORD hath proclaimed unto the end of the world, Say ye to the daughter of Zion, Behold, thy salvation cometh; behold, his reward is with him, and his work before him". (Isaiah 62:11)

At the trial when Jesus stood before the governor he asked Jesus if he was the King of the Jews. Then Jesus replied to the governor that he said so. But when Jesus was accused of the chief priests and elders he answered nothing. This was because he was there to fulfill the desire of the Father that he was to be bruised for our sins so that we may receive salvation. Pilate thought he could release Jesus if he wants to but he did not know that he could not do anything without the power given to him from heaven. Jesus said to him that Pilate had not power at all against Jesus except it were given to him from above.

"Then said Pilate unto him, Speak you not unto me? know you not that I have power to crucify you, and have power to release you? Jesus answered, You could have no power at all against me, except it were given you from above: therefore he that delivered me unto you has the greater sin". (John 19:10-11)

It was not by chance the inscription that Jesus was the 'King of Jews" was put on the cross on which Jesus was crucified but it was as God desired. Later when the chief priests asked Pilate to change the writing as "he said, I am the King of the Jews", "Pilate answered, What I have written I have written" (John 19:22) Then said the chief priests of the Jews to Pilate, Write not, The King of the Jews; but that he said, I am King of the Jews. (John 19:21) The "Kingdom of God" is not confined to only the thousand-year-reign of Lord Jesus Christ, but it has several aspects as we see in the parables recorded in Matthew Chapter 13.

Jesus did not leave behind an unconcerned attitude towards Gentiles even while he was seeking the lost sheep of Israel. The Canaanite woman, who was a Gentile, approached Jesus for a favor and although Jesus was initially reluctant to pay heed to her request he granted her request when she showed faith in him.

Leslie M. John

"And, behold, a woman of Canaan came out of the same coasts, and cried unto him, saying, Have mercy on me, O Lord, thou Son of David; my daughter is grievously vexed with a devil. But he answered her not a word. And his disciples came and besought him, saying, Send her away; for she crieth after us. But he answered and said, I am not sent but unto the lost sheep of the house of Israel. Then came she and worshipped him, saying, Lord, help me. But he answered and said, It is not meet to take the children's bread, and to cast it to dogs. And she said, Truth, Lord: yet the dogs eat of the crumbs which fall from their masters' table. Then Jesus answered and said unto her, O woman, great is thy faith: be it unto thee even as thou wilt. And her daughter was made whole from that very hour". (Matthew 15:22-28)

In another occasion when Jesus was speaking to the Samaritan woman he spoke of everlasting life. But then, she was from the descendants of Jacob mixed with Gentiles based on this verse.

"Art thou greater than our father Jacob, which gave us the well, and drank thereof himself, and his children, and his cattle?" (John 4:12)

Earlier, Jesus also spoke to a centurion and said that he had more faith than an Israelite: "When Jesus heard it, he marvelled, and said to them that followed, Verily I say unto you, I have not found so great faith, no, not in Israel". (Matthew 8:10)

That is to say that although the primary purpose of Jesus was to restore the kingdom to Children and set up 'kingdom of God' he not only showed compassion towards Gentiles while he was on this earth, but he commanded his disciples to go the regions of Jerusalem first, and then to Judea and Samaria, and then to uttermost parts of the earth to preach the Gospel of Jesus Christ. (Acts 1:8)

It is purely an assumption that Jesus never spoke to Gentiles in the Gospel of Matthew, which is basically considered as Jewish Gospel. Peter spoke of 'kingdom of God' initially as per the instructions given by Lord Jesus Christ before His ascension into heaven. He spoke to Jews first and then to Gentiles. Paul also spoke to Jews first and then to Gentiles later. Paul was chosen to speak to Gentiles, but he ventured to Jews before he

Leslie M. John

spoke to Gentiles. Some Jews accepted his message and some Jews rejected his message. This was fulfilled as was prophesied earlier. His commission is recorded in Acts 9:15

"But the Lord said unto him, Go thy way: for he is a chosen vessel unto me, to bear my name before the Gentiles, and kings, and the children of Israel"

"Make the heart of this people fat, and make their ears heavy, and shut their eyes; lest they see with their eyes, and hear with their ears, and understand with their heart, and convert, and be healed. (Isaiah 6:10)

"For the heart of this people is waxed gross, and their ears are dull of hearing, and their eyes have they closed; lest they should see with their eyes, and hear with their ears, and understand with their heart, and should be converted, and I should heal them". (Acts 28:27)

Thereafter, the message of salvation was sent out to Gentiles. This does not say that salvation message was not given out earlier than Acts 28:28 or Acts 28:31. In fact, the text in Acts 28:31 reads...

"Preaching the kingdom of God, and teaching those things which concern the Lord Jesus Christ, with all confidence, no man forbidding him" (Acts 28:31). Note here the phrase 'kingdom of God".

This does not mean that the message proclaimed at that point of time and after Acts 28:28 was only for Gentiles. This kind of interpretation leads to interpretation that the Church did not come into existence in Acts Ch. 2. Contrary to that way of interpreting, the Church indeed came into existence as we read in Acts Chapter 2. The text reads...

"Be it known therefore unto you, that the salvation of God is sent unto the Gentiles, and that they will hear it" (Acts 28:28).

The salvation of God and the message of kingdom of God that proclaimed here had the same meaning. Obviously this means that the Church began in Acts 2 when Holy Spirit came down from heaven and they who gathered there in Jerusalem waiting for Holy Spirit to come

Leslie M. John

upon them were filled with Holy Spirit. This the Baptism of Holy Spirit referred to earlier by John the Baptist in Matthew 3:11

"I indeed baptize you with water unto repentance: but he that cometh after me is mightier than I, whose shoes I am not worthy to bear: he shall baptize you with the Holy Ghost and with fire" (Matthew 3:11)

Baptism with fire is meant for those who reject salvation. They will have their part in the lake of fire along with Satan and fallen angels. It was in Acts Chapter 2 that the Church began and Jesus became the head of the Church.

According to C.I. Scofield 'kingdom of heaven' refers to the millennial kingdom of Jesus Christ and 'kingdom of God' refers to the universal, including all moral intelligences willingly subject to the will of God, whether angels, the Church, or saints of past of future dispensations 1.

 I am not comfortable with his exposition on this point. This exposition could have been accepted only if the same verses from different Gospels did not match the same theme, but it was not so. Matthew, Mark, Luke and John's Gospels used the same theme at several points using different phrases interchangeably. There are many parallel verses in the four Gospels dealing with a particular theme yet with two different phrases. Moreover, angels do not need salvation nor will fallen angels be forgiven!

 Few examples are as follows:

"From that time Jesus began to preach, and to say, Repent: for the kingdom of heaven is at hand" (Matthew 4:17)

 "And saying, The time is fulfilled, and the kingdom of God is at hand: repent ye, and believe the gospel" (Mark 1:15) "But seek ye first the kingdom of God, and his righteousness; and all these things shall be added unto you" (Matthew 6:33)

 "But rather seek ye the kingdom of God; and all these things shall be added unto you" (Luke 12:31)

Leslie M. John

"And said, Verily I say unto you, Except ye be converted, and become as little children, ye shall not enter into the kingdom of heaven" (Matthew 18:3)

"But when Jesus saw it, he was much displeased, and said unto them, Suffer the little children to come unto me, and forbid them not: for of such is the kingdom of God" (Mark 10:14)

"Verily I say unto you, Among them that are born of women there hath not risen a greater than John the Baptist: notwithstanding he that is least in the kingdom of heaven is greater than he" (Matthew 11:11)

"For I say unto you, Among those that are born of women there is not a greater prophet than John the Baptist: but he that is least in the kingdom of God is greater than he". (Luke 7:28)

Leslie M. John

# SEEK YE FIRST THE KINGDOM OF GOD

But seek you first the kingdom of God, and his righteousness; and all these things shall be added unto you. (Matthew 6:33)

As we read through the life history of Joseph, we see that he was elevated while his offenders were thrown into insecurity and fear for future. God's child, will never be left to be without hope, but will be elevated, while his offenders will be thrown in to insecurity and fear for their future. God assures his children that when they seek the Kingdom of God; all their needs will be fulfilled. Let me not get you to think that life of a child of God will be bed of roses! No! The child of God will face as many troubles as others do or even more; but there is hope that God will do everything for good for those who are called according to his purpose. Psalmist said that he has not seen any child of God begging for bread!

"I have been young, and now am old; yet have I not seen the righteous forsaken, nor his seed begging bread". (Psalms 37:25)

Those who seek pleasures of this world are not thinking in terms of securing treasures in heaven.

We see how insecure Joseph's brothers and Jacob were feeling because of their worry about future, even though they were the children of God. Seeing the circumstances around them, they were worried. Joseph's brothers felt insecure, because of their guilt feeling that God was punishing them for selling their own brother. Jacob, in his old age was worried about his children and his own future.

In fact, as we read through the story we find that everything works for good for those who are called according to his purpose.

"And we know that all things work together for good to them that love God, to them who are the called according to his purpose." Romans 8:28

It was God's plan that there should be abundance for seven years and

Leslie M. John

famine for the next seven years that should follow immediately the seven years of abundance. It was, in His plan that someone, whom he loved and thought would best fit for the disposition of food for seven years of famine, should be one from Jacob's family and that was Joseph. It was in His plan that the blessed one, Jacob, whom He called, Israel, should survive the severe famine. It was His plan that during that period of seven years of famine, someone from the family of Jacob should be in Egypt to provide food for Jacob's family.

Even when all this was happening at the behest of God, the children of Israel were worried about their survival, future, and, therefore, indicted themselves of having sold their brother, Joseph, many years ago. They did not know that their food was already stored for them by God many years before they knew about it. They were worried as to what their destiny would be.

God's children have a great a hope as we read in Matthew 6:34, where Jesus expressly, said "Take therefore no thought for the morrow: for the morrow shall take thought for the things of itself. Sufficient unto the day is the evil thereof".

Leslie M. John

# PUBLIC MINISTRY OF LORD JESUS CHRIST

"This beginning of miracles did Jesus in Cana of Galilee, and manifested forth his glory; and his disciples believed on him". John 2:11

Jesus started his ministry with the miracle that he did in Cana of Galilee, where he manifested forth his glory in order that his disciples and others there would believe that he was the Messiah. Jesus came into this world relinquishing the glory that he had with the Father and took the form of man. While on this world he lived like an ordinary man, yet with full divine power. He did miracles that were unknown to the natives of Galilee, Nazareth, Capernaum and the surrounding areas. Very few miracles are only recorded in the Scriptures.

Jesus did many miracles according to John 21:25 but very few are recorded that are sufficient for unbelievers to know about his power and glory that he had with the Father. In the miracle that Jesus did at Cana, where he turned water into wine, he manifested forth his glory. For the disciples, whom he called from the general and poor folk, to follow him, this miracle was a great consolation and rest on him in faith that he was the true Messiah. They believed on him. Jesus was walking by the Sea of Galilee, where he saw two brothers; Simon called Peter and Andrew his brother, who were casting a net into the sea to catch fishes. Jesus asked them to follow him promising that he would make them fishers of men. (Matthew 4:18-20). They immediately left their nets and followed him. This miracle that Jesus did at Cana was the first one in his ministry when he was about thirty years of age.

# SALVATION TO THE JEWS

The life of Moses contributes to an interesting study as it stands out unique in comparison with the life of Lord Jesus Christ. Moses had three major roles to perform, the first of which was to be the leader of Israelites, the second of which was to give law to the children of Israel and the third of which was to mediate between them and God.

Jesus came into this world as the way, the truth and the life, to redeem

Leslie M. John

mankind from their sinful nature. He gave the mankind the beatitudes as found in Matthew Chapter 5, 6 and 7.

Jesus gave two great commandments as recorded in Mark 12:30-31 "And thou shalt love the Lord thy God with all thy heart, and with all thy soul, and with all thy mind, and with all thy strength: this is the first commandment. And the second is like, namely this, Thou shalt love thy neighbour as thyself. There is none other commandment greater than these".

These two commandments contain the essence of all the Ten Commandments. Jesus came to be a mediator between the Father and us. Moses was the deliverer of God's children physically, while the mission of Jesus was to deliver spiritually of His people Jews first. Since Jews rejected him as Messiah the Gentiles had the privilege to approach God. But then this salvation to Gentiles was not planned all of a sudden. Apostle Paul says in Ephesians Chapter 3 and Romans chapter 11 that God's plan to give salvation to Gentiles was hidden in God from the foundation of the world and was revealed in the New Testament.

"For I would not, brethren, that ye should be ignorant of this mystery, lest ye should be wise in your own conceits; that blindness in part is happened to Israel, until the fulness of the Gentiles be come in" (Romans 11:25)

"But now hath he obtained a more excellent ministry, by how much also he is the mediator of a better covenant, which was established upon better promises". (Hebrews 8:6) The Old covenants included in them the shadows of new things to come. Old Testament law was stringent in nature, and the law demanded unconditional obedience. It was hard to keep the law that is in the Old Testament. In the New Testament God's abundant grace is available. Man by confessing his sins to God and accepting Jesus as the Lord will receive eternal life. Repentance of sins to Jesus and accepting him as the Lord is sufficient to be saved. Lord Jesus Christ is the only mediator between man and the Father.

Jesus said, in John 10:30 "I and my Father are one".

Leslie M. John

# ANTICHRIST

There is a description of Antichrist in Revelation Chapter 13. This Antichrist is not revealed to the world until the Church is taken away by the Lord and Holy Spirit is withdrawn from this world. Antichrist promises peace in the world and makes many other promises to please men. At the end of his three and half years of rule he breaks all the promises that he made and brings in hardships on the people. These hardships are the 'great tribulation'. This will last for three and half years and his regime ends.

Jesus warns in Matthew 24:4-7 about Antichrist and he instructs his disciples to be careful about the false prophets, false teachers, and also asks that they need to pray that their flight may not be in winter. He instructed them that they would hear of wars, rumors of wars, but all those things must come to pass, but still the end is not yet. Lord Jesus told them in John 16:33 that he spoke unto them these things, so that they may have peace, because in this world they would have tribulation. These tribulations are not similar to the 'great tribulation' that the Jews and the left-behind will face during the Antichrist regime. These tribulations are the ones, which every Christian will face in his/her life, when he/she is in this world. Jesus asks all of us to be comfortable because Jesus had overcome the world and he had successfully faced these kinds of tribulations on this earth.

The 'great tribulation' is different from the usual tribulations we face in our lives. Great tribulation is universal; it is not limited to a local place. It is as the world has never seen before. It would be more severe than the one that had passed by in AD 70, when many Jews were crucified upside down on the walls of Jerusalem.

"Beloved, believe not every spirit, but try the spirits whether they are of God: because many false prophets are gone out into the world. Hereby know ye the Spirit of God: Every spirit that confesseth that Jesus Christ is come in the flesh is of God: And every spirit that confesseth not that Jesus Christ is come in the flesh is not of God: and this is that spirit of antichrist, whereof ye have heard that it should come ; and even now

Leslie M. John

already is it in the world ". (1 John 4:1-3)

 John wrote about those who oppose Christ, but the description given in Revelation Chapter 13 is of the one who tries to take the position of Christ. That is of the one who would try himself to substitute in the place of Lord Jesus Christ.

For those who are left behind this 'man of sin', also known as the 'son of perdition' will appear, and he will rule over them. This Antichrist is worshipped by all those who are loyal to him and also by those who cannot tolerate the 'Great Tribulation' during that period. His number is "666 ". He forces his dictatorship to such an extent that no one can sell or buy anything unless he has a mark on his right hand or on his forehead this mark of the beast. This is one world economy. But then, there will be those who disobey him and call upon the Lord to save them. Jews will call upon the Lord to save them and the Lord helps them. These are those who are saved during great tribulation period, but they are not part of the Church and they will not have the blessings of the Church.

"Here is wisdom. Let him that hath understanding count the number of the beast: for it is the number of a man ; and his number is Six hundred threescore and six ". Revelation 13:18)

There are those who say that they do not worship any god but they will worship this beast the 'man of sin' who is also known as 'the son of perdition'. What a shame that atheists who say that they do not have god and do not worship anyone, but will worship this man, and consider him as God. There have been some shadows of this kind in the form of some religious leaders, whom people worshipped; but the real religious leader under one government in the world is yet to come. And that man cannot be seen by the Church because before his appearance the Church would have been 'caught up' into the mid-air to be with the Lord for ever and ever. The Church is the precious bride of Lord Jesus Christ and we, who are the members of the Church, will not have to see this Antichrist. Thanks to God. Note here when Antichrist and false prophet are thrown into the lake of fire! It is before the devil that deceived!!!

Does the Scripture say any body is thrown into the lake of fire before

Leslie M. John

Antichrist and false prophet? No, not at all!

At the end of the seven-year period Lord Jesus Christ with his bride, which is the Church, descends and steps on the Mount of Olives. Then follows sheep and Goat Judgment; one-thousand-year-reign of Jesus Christ; Satan being released from abyss; Satan going Gog and Magog to gather from the nations armies for himself to fight against Jesus; fire from heaven coming down and defeating Satan and his fallen angels; the resurrection of the unsaved; great white throne judgment; and casting off death, hell, Satan and his fallen angels, and all those who have not accepted Jesus as their savior into the 'lake of fire'.

"And the devil that deceived them was cast into the lake of fire and brimstone, where the beast and the false prophet are, and shall be tormented day and night for ever and ever" (Revelation 20:10). Notice that when the devil was cast into the lake of fire, the Antichrist and the false prophet were already there in the lake of fire. These are only the ones who will be in the lake of fire before the 'Great White Throne Judgment' (Revelation 16:16 and Revelation 20:8-10)

## THE THOUSAND YEAR REIGN (MILLENNIUM)

God promised Abraham that in Isaac will be the blessed people who will be His people and He will be their God. Jesus came to save the children of Israel, yet they rejected him. This paved the way for Gentiles to come to him for salvation and secure God's mercy. All those who had believed Jesus as their savior and laid faith in him were saved and all those who believe in him shall be saved. Two thieves were crucified on either side of Lord Jesus. One of them mocked Jesus while the other sought mercy from Jesus. He prayed that Jesus may remember him when He comes in his Kingdom. Jesus said to the thief who prayed for mercy that he would be in Paradise the very same day as Jesus died. Jesus was buried and rose from the dead on the third, ascended into heaven and is seated on the right hand of the Majesty. He would come soon. Salvation is available to anyone who calls upon Jesus for mercy.

Isaiah 40:11 says " He shall feed his flock like a shepherd: he shall gather the lambs with his arm, and carry [them] in his bosom, [and] shall gently lead those that are with young"

Israel has become one nation in 1948 but they do not have the shepherd yet. They rejected Jesus as their Messiah and called for his blood to be upon them. Has God forgotten Israel because they rejected him as their Messiah? No. God said "Can a woman forget her sucking child, that she should not have compassion on the son of her womb? yea, they may forget, yet will I not forget thee". Isaiah 49:15

The things are going to be worse for them that they will call for help from Jesus. He would not come until they realize that they have rejected him and they need him. They will face terrible persecution under Antichrist in the last days. They would cry that the mountains may fall on them and kill them (Rev.6:16). Israel will call upon God during the Great Tribulation period. God is not going to leave them but he will bring them on their knees to call upon his help. Then shall the Lord come to them and be their King of kings and Lord of lords. Jesus will literally reign for thousand years sitting on the throne of David.

John saw in his vision those who were martyrs for Jesus and for the word of God and also those who did not worship the Antichrist in the thousand year reign.

 Those that did not believe on Jesus did not rise from their graves. They will be thrown into the lake of fire. But, all those whose sins are washed in the blood of Jesus, irrespective of Jews or Gentiles will be caught up together to meet the Lord in the air even before the Great Tribulation starts and will be with the Lord forever. The dead shall rise first and we who are alive and remain shall be caught up together with them in the clouds to meet the Lord in the air: and so shall be ever be with the Lord. (1 Thessalonians 4:16-17)

"And I saw thrones, and they sat upon them, and judgment was given unto them: and [I saw] the souls of them that were beheaded for the witness of Jesus, and for the word of God, and which had not worshipped the beast, neither his image, neither had received [his] mark

Leslie M. John

upon their foreheads, or in their hands; and they lived and reigned with Christ a thousand years" Revelation 20:4 ";

## PETER AND JOHN TESTIFIED

While he yet spake, behold, a bright cloud overshadowed them: and behold a voice out of the cloud, which said, This is my beloved Son, in whom I am well pleased; hear ye him. (Matthew 17:5)

Peter and also the two sons of Zebedee (James and John) saw Jesus transfigured and his face shone as the sun, and his raiment was white as light, when he appeared to them. They also heard the Father saying"... This is my beloved Son, in whom I am well pleased; hear ye him..." (Matthew 17:5).

Peter was perturbed on hearing false stories about Jesus and about the unbelief about Jesus. Therefore, he testified that he and James and John witnessed the event of transfiguration of Jesus. Peter said that they did not follow cunning devised fables about Jesus; but they made known about Jesus and his glory to them as eye witnesses. Peter testified that they made known unto them the power and coming of Lord Jesus Christ.

They said that they were eye witnesses of his majesty and that they heard the voice that came down from heaven, while they were on the holy mountain. (2 Peter 1:16-18) Peter heard Jesus say that the Father loves him because he lays down his life and will take it again. (John 10:17).

John testified that "the Word was made flesh, and dwelt among us, (and we beheld his glory, the glory as of the only begotten of the Father,) full of grace and truth". (John 1:14)

True, we enjoy the benefits of the love of God because Jesus laid down his life our sake; "But God raised him from the dead" (Acts 13:30). We are cleansed of our sins by the blood of Jesus Christ shed on the cross. This is the truth and faith in him alone saves a person from damnation.

Leslie M. John

Do not trust every spirit, but test the sprits to know for yourself whether or not those spirits are of God. There are many false prophets and preachers gone out into this world. The way to know whether someone is from the living God or not is to make sure whether or not that person confesses that Jesus Christ is the incarnation of the Father and dwelt among us. Anyone, who does not confess that Jesus is come in the flesh, is not of God but of antichrist. There are many out there now who say that a man can gain salvation by good works. It is time we know them and realize that they are not from God.

If you are not yet saved, here is word from Apostle Paul, who says that if you confess with your mouth the Lord Jesus and believe in your heart that God raised him from the dead you shall be saved. (Romans 10:9)

## STREET OF GOLD

"And the twelve gates were twelve pearls; every several gate was of one pearl: and the street of the city was pure gold, as it were transparent glass". (Revelation 21:21)

In this secular world we see the importance of gold. What if we who are common people in this world can tread on a street of gold, and live in a city made of the most precious metals?
Bible speaks of such precious metals, which even common man tread on, and live in a city made of most precious metals. Revelation chapter 21 presents the most beautiful city and the inhabitants there in.

John saw in his vision the holy city, New Jerusalem, coming down out of heaven from God, prepared for a bride, who was adorned for her husband. The description is great. Who is this bride? Bible speaks of the bride as the Church/Assembly constituting the believers in Christ, the saved ones. The bride is adorned waiting for her husband to come and here is the chaste virgin, adorned waiting for the New Jerusalem.

The tabernacle is referred to in the Old Testament, as the sacred tent in which God came and dwelt. Here in this chapter John saw God himself coming down and dwelling among his people, who will be his people,

Leslie M. John

and he will be their God, who will wipe away all their tears, and there will be no more death, nor sorrow, nor crying, no more pain, because all the old things have passed away by then.

It is the new heaven where the Assembly/Church, constituting the saved ones, which is his bride, will dwell.

Isaiah 65:17 presents the prophecy about the new heavens and a new earth that will be created and about the former earth and heaven which will pass away and will not be remembered.

In Revelation 21:1 we read that city, which is beautiful and which has no sea, but only the inhabitants, who are always happy and without any sufferings. . Rev 21: 18 "And the building of the wall of it was of jasper: and the city was pure gold, like unto clear glass"

 Our savior Jesus Christ has undergone severe pain when men pierced sword in to his body and beat him. He was crowned with a crown of thorns and blood and water gushed forth from the side of his body. It is through that blood of Jesus Christ that we are saved. He suffered on the cross of Calvary that so that we may have eternal life. It is through the shedding of his precious blood that our sins are cleansed and through that blood of Christ that our filth is cleansed and we are made clear as crystal. That city of precious metals is prepared for us."

But for those who do not accept Jesus Christ as their personal Savior, there is another place designated and it is the lake of fire, as we read in Rev. 21: 8. It is described as the "lake which burneth with fire and brimstone" which is the second death.

 And I saw no temple in it: for the Lord God Almighty and the Lamb are the temple of it. And the city had no need of the sun, neither of the moon, to shine in it: for the glory of God is its light, and the Lamb is its lamp. (Revelation 21:22-23)

Leslie M. John

# PILLARS IN HEAVEN

Pillars are the strength of monuments and on the pillars are seen inscriptions or designs that either bring to us some remembrance of those, who responsibly raised them, or help us admire their beauty. Heaven does not need any pillar to support it, but the new Jerusalem, that John saw in his vision coming down from heaven was like a bride adorned for her bridegroom. In this new Jerusalem were seen the pillars on which were written the names of those, who served the living God and the name of the God whom they served. Some in the Church at Philadephia had not defiled their garments and they were worthy to receive blessings. God promised that he who overcomes shall walk with Him (Rev 3:3-5).

This is the difference between the earthly Jerusalem and the new Jerusalem that comes down from heaven. John saw a new heaven and a new earth after the first heaven and the first earth passed away and there was no more sea. In this new Jerusalem there was not seen any difference between Jews or Gentiles, but those who were there were all one in Christ. They had put on righteousness of Christ as their garments. They had received Jesus as their personal Savior and Lord by grace through faith in him.

More than anyone taking airs of his belonging to any clan the important fact that is to be borne in mind is that it is the grace of God that saves a man. No man needs precious metals such as gold or silver to earn a place in new Jerusalem, but all that a man needs is to have simple faith in Jesus, the Son of God and make him Lord of his/her life. God wipes away their tears. There shall be no more death, no more sorrow, no more crying and no more pain.

God shall give freely to all that thirst for such a life the fountain of life. He who overcomes the world and the temptations therein shall inherit the blessings from God and he shall be His son.(Rev. 21:2-7)

Leslie M. John

## JERUSALEM WILL BE
## CALLED BY A NEW NAME

The Holy city Jerusalem, the city of our Lord, is now desolate and not in good shape. The city is forsaken and destroyed. But, the day will come when the city will be called "Hephzibah", and its land "Beulah". The Lord delights in making the city delightful for every one and the land like married woman. (Isaiah Ch. 62:4). This is a prophecy about the status of Jerusalem in the millennial kingdom of Jesus.

Lord Jesus Christ is the Messiah. The Jews rejected him and called upon them the blood of Jesus in order that he may be crucified (Matthew 27:24-25). Peter's speech testifies about those who crucified Jesus.

"Ye men of Israel, hear these words; Jesus of Nazareth, a man approved of God among you by miracles and wonders and signs, which God did by him in the midst of you, as ye yourselves also know: Him, being delivered by the determinate counsel and foreknowledge of God, ye have taken, and by wicked hands have crucified and slain" (Acts 2:22-23)

Indeed, they paid the price in AD 70 according to historians. Earlier, they worshipped idols many-a-time and were chastised by God. They rebelled against God and paid the price for their actions. Yet, they are his people; the city of David is his city.

Like Boaz, who was kinsman redeemer of Ruth, Jesus is our redeemer. He came into this world, died for our sins, was buried, rose from the dead on the third day and later ascended into heaven. He is seated on the right hand of the Majesty and interceding for us. We, who are redeemed by the blood of Christ, are greater than the unrepentant Jews. But for those, who have accepted Jesus as their personal savior, there is no condemnation irrespective of their race, ethnicity, color, or creed.

Lord Jesus, who is the messiah, speaks and says that he will not sit quite, nor will he rest until he redeems city of Jerusalem again. He defeats the kings loyal to Antichrist at "Armageddon", and sits on the throne of

Leslie M. John

David and literally rules. In the thousand years of his rule there shall be perfect peace. Satan will be bound with chains and thrown into abyss by an angel who comes from heaven. Later Satan will be released for a short time when he goes Gog and Magog to deceive the nations but fire from God comes down from heaven and devours Satan. (Revelation Ch. 20:8) The dead who did not accept Jesus Christ as their personal savior will resurrect at that time.

The Lord shall judge them at the 'Great white throne' and cast them along with death, hell, and the devil and his angels into the 'lake of fire' to be tormented for ever and ever. This is the second death. For those who are saved, there is no second death but they will have everlasting life to be with the Lord for ever and ever. Note here when Antichrist and false prophet are thrown into the lake of fire! It is before the devil that deceived!!! Revelation 20:10 confirms it.

When the devil was cast into the lake of fire, the Antichrist and the false prophet were already there in the lake of fire. These are only the ones who will be in the lake of fire before the 'Great White Throne Judgment' (Revelation 16:16 and Revelation 20:8-10). Do Scriptures say that anybody was thrown into the lake of fire or will be thrown into lake of fire before Antichrist and false prophet? No! They are the first one to be thrown into lake of fire.

There shall come out of heaven a New Jerusalem and we, who are saved, shall be in that Holy City. The Church is the bride of our Lord Jesus Christ. Lord Jesus says that he has set watchmen upon the walls of Jerusalem and they will not keep quite nor will sleep but keep a watch over the city and will make the city a praise of the earth. This is a promise of Messiah and he has sworn by his right hand and by the arm of his strength. Messiah promised that no more the enemies of Jerusalem will eat its corn as their food no stranger will ever drink its wine. Gentiles will see its righteousness and kings will glory.

"And the Gentiles shall see thy righteousness, and all kings thy glory: and thou shalt be called by a new name, which the mouth of the LORD shall name." (Isaiah 62:2)

Leslie M. John

------------------------------------------------------------------------

Bibliography:
Scofield, C. I. "Scofield Reference Notes on Matthew 6". "Scofield
Reference Notes (1917 Edition)".
<http://www.studylight.org/com/srn/view.cgi?book=mt&chapter=006>.
1917)

http://www.studylight.org/his/bc/wfj/antiquities
http://www.biblestudytools.com/history/flavius-josephus/antiquities-
jews/book-1/chapter-6.html

Leslie M. John

# CHAPTER 12
# JESUS SAVES YOU

JESUS SAID "Except a man be born again, he cannot see the kingdom of God"

What does it mean to be born-again?

"Jesus answered and said unto him, Verily, verily, I say unto thee, Except a man be born again, he cannot see the kingdom of God. Nicodemus saith unto him, How can a man be born when he is old? can he enter the second time into his mother's womb, and be born? Jesus answered, Verily, verily, I say unto thee, Except a man be born of water and of the Spirit, he cannot enter into the kingdom of God". (John 3:3-5)

Jesus Christ died for our sins; he rose from the dead and ascended into heaven. He is now seated at the right hand of the Majesty and He is coming again soon.

## SIN CONQURED MAN

Holy Bible says God created man in his own image. God planted a garden eastward in Eden and he put there the man whom God called Adam. The garden was indeed beautiful with every tree pleasant to sight and good for food. The LORD God made every tree to grow from the ground, the tree of life also in the midst of the garden, and the tree of knowledge of good and evil. The LORD God put the man into the Garden of Eden to dress it and keep it. He said to the man that he may freely eat of every tree of the garden but of the tree of knowledge of good and evil he shall not eat; and in the day he eats it he shall surely die. God saw that man was alone and the LORD God said that the man should not be alone. He decided to give a "help meet" for man.

The LORD God caused a deep sleep upon Adam and while he was sleeping God took one of the ribs of the man and made a woman out of

Leslie M. John

the rib and brought to him. Adam called her as "Woman" because she was taken out of Man. God said to the man to be fruitful, multiply, replenish the earth, and subdue it and have dominion over the fish of the sea, fowl of the air and every living thing that moves on the earth. (Genesis 2:8-28).

## SATAN DECEIVED MAN

The serpent, who was more subtle than any other beast of the field, deceived the woman with his enticing words. The serpent spoke to her and convinced her that God did not tell the truth. The woman yielded to the temptation of the serpent. She saw that the tree was good for food and pleasure for the eyes and thought the tree would give her intelligence. She took of its fruit and ate and also gave to her husband and he ate it. The eyes of both of them opened and they knew that they were naked. They made aprons for themselves with fig-leaves and when they heard the voice of God, whose name is "Jehovah Elohim" they hid themselves from his presence.

Jehovah Elohim called man and asked him where he was? The man said he feared because he was naked and hid himself. God demanded an answer from the man as to who said to him that he was naked and questioned if he had he eaten fruit of the tree that he was asked not to eat from! The man blamed woman and the woman blamed the serpent.

## THE CURSE FROM GOD FOLLOWED

The LORD God cursed the earth for man; the woman with pain in her child labor, and God cursed serpent that the serpent would crawl all the days of his life. This resulted in Adam toiling for food; woman who was in Adam and who became his wife to be a help-mate was cursed with pain in her child-bearing. The serpent who was not crawling before became a most loathed reptile on the earth to crawl on the earth his entire life. God put enmity between the seed of the woman and of the serpent. Adam called the woman as "Eve" because she was the mother of all living. This is how the sin entered the world. In order to reconcile man to God, Jesus relinquished his glory in heaven and came down into this

Leslie M. John

world in the form of man and lived among us.

"And I will put enmity between thee and the woman, and between thy seed and her seed; it shall bruise thy head, and thou shalt bruise his heel". (Genesis 3:15)

# GOD SENT HIS ONLY BEGOTTEN SON

"For God so loved the world, that he gave his only begotten Son, that whosoever believeth in him should not perish, but have everlasting life" (John 3:16)
Jesus said: "Therefore doth my Father love me, because I lay down my life, that I might take it again". (John 10:17)

## SALVATION IS FREE OF COST

According to Bible good works alone will not get us into heaven but faith in Lord Jesus Christ alone saves us. Confession by mouth and the belief that God raised Him from the dead will get us salvation free of cost. Salvation is free. No amount of good works can get a person a place in heaven. The works will follow faith in Jesus Christ and salvation. May the Word of God speak to our hearts

Heavenly Father's love is shown in John Chapter 3:16. He sent His only begotten Son, Jesus Christ for our sake that whosoever believes in him should not perish but have everlasting life. There is a clause which is conditional here. The condition is that a person has to believe that The Father has sent His only begotten Son, Jesus Christ into this world for the remission of our sins. The purpose of sending Jesus into this world was that whoever believes in Him through Jesus Christ he will have everlasting life.

The initial mission of Jesus was to seek the lost sheep of Israel. Jesus also said to his twelve disciples not to go into the way of the Gentiles and into any city of Samaritans. This was the time when Jesus preached the Kingdom of heaven (Matthew 10:5-6). Later in Mathew Chapter 15 we

Leslie M. John

see that a Gentile woman from Canaan approached Jesus and prayed to him addressing him as "O Lord, thou Son of David" and crying out to have mercy on her because her daughter was grievously vexed with a devil. Jesus did not answer her testing her faith but when his disciples interceded to send her away because she was crying, Jesus answered and said he was not sent but unto the lost sheep of the house of the Israel. This should not be misunderstood that Jesus came into this world only for the sake of Jews. It is indeed true that his first priority was to seek the lost sheep of Israel.

Until his crucifixion Jesus was under the Law of Moses. It was divine plan that Jesus should keep the Law of Moses meticulously; yet Jesus being the Son of God, had compassion on the Gentile woman that her faith was great and granted to her answer to her prayer and her daughter was made whole from that very hour. (Matthew 15:22-28). Jesus nailed the handwritten laws and ordinances of Moses at the cross because they were contrary to the Gentiles. Those ordinances were blotted out as Apostle Paul wrote in Colossians 2:14. The message of Salvation is sent out to everyone on the earth after resurrection of Jesus Christ as per the commission given by Jesus in Matthew Chapter 28:19-20 and Acts 1:8

David wrote in Psalm 28:1 "Unto thee will I cry, O LORD my rock; be not silent to me: lest, if thou be silent to me, I become like them that go down into the pit" God will answer our prayers when we pray with faith. In the Gospel according to John Chapter 10 God's love is shown toward all those who believe in him. There is a security of salvation assured. Jesus is the Good Shepherd. Jesus said: "Therefore doth my Father love me, because I lay down my life, that I might take it again". (John 10:17). The believer in Christ is not redeemed with corruptible things such as silver and gold or from vain conversations of forefathers but by the precious blood of Lord Jesus Christ. (1 Peter 1:18) God had sent Jesus Christ to be a propitiation for us and whoever believes in him shall be redeemed of his sin and justified before him. (Romans 3:25, 1 John 2:2)

"Herein is love, not that we loved God, but that he loved us, and sent his Son to be the propitiation for our sins".1 John 4:10

Leslie M. John

"In whom we have redemption through his blood, the forgiveness of sins, according to the riches of his grace; Ephesians 1:7

"And that he might reconcile both unto God in one body by the cross, having slain the enmity thereby" Ephesians 2:16

"In whom we have redemption through his blood, even the forgiveness of sins" Colossians 1:14
"And, having made peace through the blood of his cross, by him to reconcile all things unto himself; by him, I say, whether they be things in earth, or things in heaven". Colossians 1:20

God loved us first and not that we did first. That is the reason why, though we trespassed His commandments, He sent His one and only Son, Jesus Christ to die on our stead.

## JESUS CONQURED SATAN

"So Christ was once offered to bear the sins of many; and unto them that look for him shall he appear the second time without sin unto salvation". Hebrews 9:28

"That if thou shalt confess with thy mouth the Lord Jesus, and shalt believe in thine heart that God hath raised him from the dead, thou shalt be saved". Romans 10:9

"Whom God hath raised up, having loosed the pains of death: because it was not possible that he should be holden of it". (Acts 2:24)

"But ye shall receive power, after that the Holy Ghost is come upon you: and ye shall be witnesses unto me both in Jerusalem, and in all Judaea, and in Samaria, and unto the uttermost part of the earth. And when he had spoken these things, while they beheld, he was taken up; and a cloud received him out of their sight. And while they looked stedfastly toward heaven as he went up, behold, two men stood by them in white apparel; Which also said, Ye men of Galilee, why stand ye gazing up into heaven? this same Jesus, which is taken up from you into heaven, shall so come in like manner as ye have seen him go into heaven." (Acts 1:8-11)

Leslie M. John

Jesus died for our sake; he was buried, and was raised from the dead. Jesus, who is the seed of the woman, crushed the head of the serpent at the cross. Jesus rose from the dead on the third day and he appeared to many. Death could not hold him in the grave and He conquered death. Later after forty days he ascended into heaven. Jesus will come again in the same manner he ascended into heaven.

# TAKE REFUGE IN
# THE LIVING GOD

This meditation is about two individuals in the war between Philistines and the children of Israel at a land that belonged to Judah. The first one was Goliath, who was proud, huge, tall, strong man from Philistines. The second one was David, the son of Jesse, who belonged to the children of Israel.

Philistines took pride in their leader Goliath in the battle at Shochloh, which beloged to Judah. Saul and men of Israel gathered on the other side by the valley of Elah. Philistines stood on a mountain on one side and the Israel stood on a mountain on the other side (1 Samuel 17:1-3)

Saul was the first king of Israel. He was the son of Kish from the tribe of Benjamin. He was young, handsome and taller than any one among the children of Israel. (1 Samuel 9:1-2)

There was no response to Goliath's challenge either from Saul or anyone from Israel until the ruddy shepherd David came along to take up the challenge. Goliath looked upon David with scorn and shouted. Goliath ridiculed the God of Israel and wondered if David thought that Goliath was a dog! He boasted in his gods and said that he would give David's flesh to the fowls of the air and to the beasts of the field.

The response from David who hoped in the Almighty and living God was equally challenging. David honored the living God when he said to Goliath that he was facing the mighty man in the name of the Lord of hosts, the God of armies of Israel, whom Goliath defied.

"Then said David to the Philistine, Thou comest to me with a sword, and with a spear, and with a shield: but I come to thee in the name of the LORD of hosts, the God of the armies of Israel, whom thou hast defied. This day will the LORD deliver thee into mine hand; and I will smite thee, and take thine head from thee; and I will give the carcases of the host of the Philistines this day unto the fowls of the air, and to the wild beasts of the earth; that all the earth may know that there is a God in Israel". (1 Samuel 17:45-46)

Goliath arose, went to meet David in the battlefield, and drew close, like a stalking mountain, overlaid with brass and iron. David advanced with greater strength in God and cheerfulness, as one that aimed more to execute God's command rather than to make a figure: He hasted, and ran, was being lightly clad, to meet the Philistine. Before honor is humility. David put one of the pebbles in the sling and hurled at Goliath. There it was! The pebble struck straight at Goliath's forehead and in the twinkling of an eye, it fetched him to the ground. Goliath fell with his face down on the ground.

"Therefore David ran, and stood upon the Philistine, and took his sword, and drew it out of the sheath thereof, and slew him, and cut off his head therewith. And when the Philistines saw their champion was dead, they fled". (1 Samuel 17:51)

## TRUST IN THE LORD

Jesus walked on water. Peter was about to sink because he feared the tumultuous wind.  as long as Peter looked unto Jesus he was able to walk on the water just as Jesus himself was walking on the water, but when Peter feared seeing the wind boisterous he started sinking. Peter, then, called upon his savior to save him. Jesus immediately stretched forth his hand and lifted Peter from sinking.

"But when he saw the wind boisterous, he was afraid; and beginning to sink, he cried, saying, Lord, save me. And immediately Jesus stretched

Leslie M. John

forth his hand, and caught him, and said unto him, O thou of little faith, wherefore didst thou doubt? " Matthew 14:30-31

Jesus sent away multitudes of men, woman and children, whom he fed with five loaves and two fishes, and moved into a desert place. This was after he heard that John was beheaded. Jesus asked his disciples to go by ship to the other side of the sea and he went up into a mountain to pray until the evening. He was all alone there but the ship was in the midst of the sea and the strong winds blew and sea tossed with waves. Jesus went toward the ship in the night.

The disciples saw Jesus walking on the water and coming toward them, but they feared that it was a spirit and cried. It was then that Jesus their savior told them to be of good cheer and said it was he, who was walking toward them. Peter was eager to walk on water. Peter asked Jesus if Jesus could call him to walk on water toward him. When Peter sought help to go near to him Jesus said to him 'come down out the ship '.

As Peter was making endeavors to walk toward Jesus he saw that the wind was boisterous, and got frightened. As soon as Peter got frightened he started sinking and cried to Jesus saying "Lord, save me ". Jesus did not leave Peter helpless, but immediately stretched forth his hand and caught him. Jesus admonished Peter of his little faith. Seeing that Peter was failing Jesus questioned him as to why he doubted. Peter's doubt and fear brought failure to himself, but as soon as he called out for help from Jesus he readily helped Peter. When they came into the ship the wind stopped. Then all those who were in the ship came and worshipped him, saying that Jesus was the Son of God.

Doubt causes fear resulting in loss of faith and yet when calling on God will bring success. Give God a chance to work in you, rather than having alternate plans to work for yourself with your own wisdom and strength. Psalmist says - "Some trust in chariots, and some in horses: but we will remember the name of the LORD our God ". (Psalms 20:7)";

"And we know that all things work together for good to them that love God, to them who are the called according to his purpose". (Romans 8:28)

Leslie M. John

The children of Israel had reached the borders of the Promised land and it would not take many days to get into the land. But at that time the LORD spoke to Moses saying that he should send men one from each tribe of their fathers to the Promised land of Canaan and spy out the land and see if the people living there were strong or weak, few or many, whether the land was good or bad, whether the cities they live in were tents or strong holds, whether or not the land was rich or poor, whether or not there was wood and then commanded them to be of good courage and bring of the fruit of the land. He also suggested that the grapes were ripe then. (Numbers 13:1-2, Numbers 13:17-20)

A quick reading of this chapter will surely render misunderstanding that it was God's plan to send the spies to the land of Canaan and check it out whether the land of Canaan was really good or not. But it was not so. God did not need to check the strength of the men who were living in Canaan. God knew that the land which He promised to the children of Israel was very good one and it was a land where milk and honey was flowing. The land was rich in fruit, wood and cities were strong.

God promised the best for the children of Israel and there was no need for Him to send spies to search the land that He may change His promise. No, it was not so. It was the request of the children of Israel that the LORD was responding to. God had already promised the Israelites that the land of Canaan was given to them for their possession. All that they had to do was to believe on the LORD and go forward to possess it.

"Behold, the LORD thy God hath set the land before thee: go up and possess it, as the LORD God of thy fathers hath said unto thee; fear not, neither be discouraged". (Deuteronomy 1:21)

But the children of Israel had been murmuring from the time they left Egypt until they reached the borders of the Promised Land. They were at Kadeshbarnea, which was very close to the Promised Land of Canaan (Deuteronomy 1:19); but then it was they who decided that they would send spies to search the land and bring them report. That is to say that they did not depend on God's word but wanted to depend on the report which their own men would present to them and consider whether or not they should enter the Promised land of Canaan.

Leslie M. John

The children of Israel murmured against Moses and the LORD and felt that their journey in the wilderness was not worth leaving the land of Egypt (Deuteronomy 1:22-27) Thus they displeased the LORD many a time on their journey. Their mindset was still of slavery even when they were at the borders of the land of Canaan. They did not trust the LORD in spite of seeing miraculous protection they had all through their journey; they never lacked food or water, yet they murmured against the LORD and worshipped idols on their journey from Egypt to Canaan.

"And ye murmured in your tents, and said, Because the LORD hated us, he hath brought us forth out of the land of Egypt, to deliver us into the hand of the Amorites, to destroy us". (Deuteronomy 1:27)

Hebrews 11:1 says: "Now faith is the substance of things hoped for, the evidence of things not seen".

Here in this particular situation we see that the children of Israel failed in faith and tempted God. They did not trust that God, who promised them the land of Canaan, would be really the God worth believing. They did not believe that the land of Canaan was really the land where milk and honey was flowing. God gave them the promise that this rich land will be given to them for their possession. It was given even when they were still under the bondage of slavery (Exodus 3:8). God delivered them from the bondage under Pharaoh and led them through the wilderness unto the borders of Canaan, where they stopped to murmur again losing their faith in God. It was as if they would decide for themselves whether or not they want to enter the land of Canaan. The promise was about to be fulfilled when the children of Israel had doubted God's promise and reaped the consequences.

Once again, God agreed to their request and said to Moses that he should send twelve men one from each of the tribe of their fathers to spy out and bring the news. The LORD agreed that they may really see if God's word was right. Moses sent twelve men as commanded. As we read further in Numbers Chapters 13 and 14 we see that the children of Israel paid the price for their unbelief and rebellion against the LORD.

Let us trust God that He will always do well to us.

Leslie M. John

"There is therefore now no condemnation to them which are in Christ Jesus, who walk not after the flesh, but after the Spirit". (Romans 8:1)

"Behold, the LORD thy God hath set the land before thee: go up [and] possess [it], as the LORD God of thy fathers hath said unto thee; fear not, neither be discouraged" Deuteronomy 1:21

The twelve men chosen as spies to spy out the land of Canaan searched the land and returned to their camp after forty days. Except Joshua, the son of Nun and Caleb, the son of Jephunneh, the other ten men gave report and suggested not to enter the land of Canaan. Everyone of the twelve gave report but the ten men (other than Joshua and Caleb) gave a report filled with disbelief, cowardice and fear. They showed the fruit of the land, especially a branch with one cluster of grapes, which was carried by two of them on a staff, and of pomegranates and of the figs. Any one who saw vineyard would know that a cluster of grapes on branch does not require two men to carry it on a staff, but the cluster of grapes that they picked up from the brook of Eshcol in the land of Canaan was so big that it needed two men to carry it on a staff.. Indeed, this shows that the land was plenteous in good fruit. This was the land that God promised to the children of Israel. (Numbers 13:23-24)

The ten men who gave evil report of the land of Canaan said to Moses that the land was indeed very good and it surely flowed with milk and honey but the men, who were living there were giants and strong. The report was filled with facts about the abundance and those facts were true. The report was corroborating with God's assurance of the abundance in that land. God told them about it even when they were still under the bondage in Egypt. The facts about the land that their report presented did not change the truth that God told them earlier. God knew it earlier and promised the land to them for their possession. But as they came to the borders of the land of Promised land they doubted and wanted to spy out the land and have conviction that God's saying was really so. What a disbelief they had! It was God who promised the land with milk and honey flowing but they chose to confirm if the truth that God said to them was really so. They trusted in their own strength and wisdom rather than God's promise.

Leslie M. John

The ten men not only presented an evil report but presented along with the report great discouragement, and fear. As they were journeying in the wilderness for forty years they saw God's power in defeating their enemies, yet, when they saw giants in the land of Canaan they were afraid. They saw the children of Anak, Amalekites on the south, Httites, Jebusites, and Amorites in the mountain region and Canaanites by the sea and by the cost of Jordan. They said that they felt like grasshoppers before those giants and, therefore, suggested to Moses that the children of Israel should not venture entering the land of Canaan. They have put all their efforts of their travel from Egypt to the borders of Canaan into the purview of pessimism. They lost faith in God and trusted in their own strength. Whereas the giants would have been made like grasshoppers before the children of Israel if they truly depended on God, now the giants in their sight appeared huge. They felt that they were like grasshoppers before the giants. Fear brings disappointment and loss of faith in the one who promised better things. They lost faith in the strength of the Almighty and feared them because they were huge. (Numbers 13:33)

Nevertheless, Caleb and Joshua were not of that spirit of cowardice, but of full of faith and courage. They spoke to Moses and encouraged him to go forward to possess the land that flowed with milk and honey. They saw the fruit of the land that it was good and the huge physical structure of the giants of that land did not bring disappointment or fear in them. Caleb said "Let us go up at once, and possess it, for we are well able to overcome it" (Numbers 13:30).

As we read Numbers Chapter 14 we see that the children of Israel stoned Moses and wanted to go back to Egypt from where they came. Moses was protected by divine power and no danger came upon him but ponder over the rebellion in the minds of the children of Israel. They decided to choose another captain for them and return to the land of Egypt where they served as slaves. They were freed by God, yet they were trying to choose to return to that slavery. They saw the mighty power of God, wonderful protection of God and they had sumptuous food and sweet water on their journey. They had the presence of God with them when He came down and dwelt among them in the

Leslie M. John

Tabernacle, yet they were afraid when they saw the giants.

This is the condition of many believers even now. Fear encompasses their minds resulting in loss of faith and increase in disappointment. But God wants us not to return to the slavery under sin but be of good courage and fruitful to him. God blesses those who rejoice in Him. God is loving and long-suffering. Jesus is standing at the door of your heart and knocking at your door. If you will, He will enter in and dwell there. There are number of references in the New Testament for believers in Christ to have faith in Jesus that they may live a life of sufficiency, and of peace without any fear.

In Matthew 6:30 Jesus asks if God can clothe the grass of the field that does not live long how much more God can clothe the believers who depend on him. That was an assurance from him that the believers in him do not need to worry as to how they would be clothed, but seek the kingdom of God first.

In Matthew 8:10 Jesus marveled at the faith of a Gentile Centurion who believed in Jesus and sought that his servant who lay with sick of palsy and grievously tormented may be healed. Jesus marveled that even in Israel he did not see such great faith and said to the Centurion "Go thy way; and as thou hast believed, so be it done unto thee. And his servant was healed in the selfsame hour" (Matthew 8:13)

In Matthew 8:26 we see that the disciples of Jesus were afraid when they saw the tempest in the sea while they were sailing in a ship. They prayed to Jesus to save them that they may not perish. Jesus wondered at their lack of faith and asked them as to why they were fearful, and called them "O ye of little faith", and then he arose and rebuked the winds and the sea. The winds and the sea obeyed him and the sea calmed down. The men marveled that even the winds and the sea obey Jesus.

The same Jesus is asking us to trust him that he may be with us always and help us. If we trust him he will give us peace not as the world gives, but He gives us His peace.

"Peace I leave with you, my peace I give unto you: not as the world

Leslie M. John

giveth, give I unto you. Let not your heart be troubled, neither let it be afraid" John 14:27.

# DO NOT FEAR GIANTS

But the very hairs of your head are all numbered. (Matthew 10:30)
Is it not wonderful that our God knows us not only by our names but by every detail that is in us including the number of hairs on our head. He has count of them and yet we stumble in faith several times. It is our weakness that we fail to understand the mighty power of God and his provision for us. However, we should be aware of the fact that if we neglect or doubt his care for us we will reap the consequences of our disbelief and run into loss.

The children of Israel stumbled upon their faith in the Lord and paid severely for their lack of faith. They feared that the giants whom their representatives saw were capable of harming them whereas God said no weapon formed against them will prosper. Every one of the age above twenty years including Moses and Aaron, except Joshua and Caleb, died before they reached the Promised Land of Canaan. The details are in Numbers chapter 14

On hearing the evil report from the ten spies the congregation cried whole night and murmured against Moses and Aaron. The congregation asked Moses and Aaron if God wanted them to die in the wilderness and asked why they were moved out of Egypt with the promise that they would have a better life! Then after hearing the evil report from the ten they preferred to go back to slavery in Egypt rather than die in the wilderness. This was their disappointment because of their lack of faith in God who promised them the land flowing with milk and honey.

This was the result of their lack of belief in God who gave them protection from rain and heat. They never lacked food, nor did their shoe wear out during their entire journey for forty years. But they believed the discouraging evil report of the ten men who went out to make a survey of the land. They sent their emissaries to make their own choice despite God's promise that he would bless them with land that had abundance.

Leslie M. John

Their own witnesses brought a cluster of grapes hanging on a staff carried by two men from that land to them to see, yet when they heard that there were Anakites, who were giants they lost faith.

Perhaps, they thought their God was smaller than the giants their men saw in the land. The men felt that they were like grasshoppers before the giants in spite of the fact that they defeated mighty kings on their journey with the help of God. Now that the children of Israelites were entrapped in their own false beliefs and lack of faith in God, they forged forward to kill Moses and Aaron, who were interceding on behalf of them to God all through their journey.

The children of Israel were making a decision to choose a captain to lead them back to Egypt from where they came to Kadeshbarnea, which was so close to the Promised Land. They wanted to go back from blessings to curse and lead a life of slavery in a sinful land once again. Earlier, when they were in Egypt crying to God for help and prayed that they may be delivered from the slavery, God heard their cry and redeemed them from the bondage of slavery under Pharaoh. Until God executed the last plague of killing the firstborn of Egyptians, Pharaoh did not allow them to leave Egypt. Israelites saw that their own firstborn were spared by God, yet now listening to disappointing evil report they changed their mind. How feeble and frail was their mind that they lost faith in their God and believed in the evil report.

Moses, who interceded on their behalf several times, fell once again face down before the congregation of all the children of Israel to cry to the Lord. Aaron accompanied Moses in his prayers and Joshua and Caleb tore down their clothes to support Moses and Aaron.

God heard their prayer and promised them pardon yet their earthly blessings of possessing the land of Canaan were lost to them in their time. That land which was with milk and honey flowing was promised to them for their possession but all those who started their journey from Egypt, except Joshua and Caleb and those who were below the age of twenty years, perished in the wilderness.

If you are not yet saved this is the day for accepting Jesus as your

Leslie M. John

personal savior. Do not fear any adversity. You are of more value than many sparrows, who toil not, yet they have their food and protection every day. If you are saved already, then never fear those who have the authority over your flesh but fear the one who has the authority over body, soul and spirit. Jesus said he has overcome this world. He is Lord Jesus Christ who is the only savior. Salvation of a believer is never lost, yet believer should live a holy life always.

"Fear ye not therefore, ye are of more value than many sparrows. Whosoever therefore shall confess me before men, him will I confess also before my Father which is in heaven" (Matthew 10:31-32)

## TRUST GOOD REPORT

"Finally, brethren, whatsoever things are true, whatsoever things are honest, whatsoever things are just, whatsoever things are pure, whatsoever things are lovely, whatsoever things are of good report; if there be any virtue, and if there be any praise, think on these things". (Philippians 4:8)

Apostle Paul writes in his epistle to Philippians that they should rejoice in the Lord, and not be worried of anything; rather submit their prayers and supplications to God. He also advises that whatsoever things are true, honest, pure, and lovely and whatsoever are of good report and if there is any virtue in them, then they should consider them as acceptable.

Of the twelve men who went to spy the land of Canaan and bring report of it, ten brought a report that presented a true picture of the abundance in the land, yet they were afraid of the giants. Even though their report was true of the abundance of the land yet their report of the men in that land was evil. They presented a very poor picture of their own strength against the giants they saw in the land of Canaan. They forgot that God's strength was always there with them and yet they were afraid of the giants in the Promised Land.

Of the twelve men who went to spy the land of Canaan and bring report of it, two brought a report that presented not only a true picture of the abundance of that land but they gave an excellent report of their own strength in the Lord and faith that they can defeat the giants in the land of Canaan. The two men who presented a good report were Joshua, the son of Nun and Caleb, the son of Jephunneh.

Joshua and Caleb gave an encouraging and a true report to Moses and Aaron and all the congregation of the Israel, of the land of Canaan and said that the land that they saw was exceedingly good. Their faith was in the living God and said if God was pleased he would give the land to them. They requested that the congregation be patient and not rebel against their leaders. They said to the people that there is no need to be afraid of the giants in the land of Canaan that all the twelve men saw. They gave assurance that the giants in that land of Canaan will be made like bread for them when God makes it possible for them to tread on their land and advised them not to fear. They repeated that the defense of the giants is gone and the LORD was with Israel.

In spite of all the assurances from Joshua and Caleb and Moses and Aaron falling in obeisance to them requesting them to pay heed to the LORD and them, the congregation stoned them. It was at this time that the glory of the LORD appeared in the tabernacle of the congregation before all the children of Israel. The LORD spoke and said to Moses of His disapproval of the cry of the children of Israel. The LORD asked how long these people kept on provoking Him and how long would it be before they fully trusted the LORD. The LORD showed signs and miracles among them, yet they rebelled against Him. The LORD was very angry on the children of Israel and said that He will smite them with pestilence and disinherit them.

The consequence of their disobedience was very serious. All those who were above the age of twenty years including Moses and Aaron, who disobeyed God at some point in their life, did not have the privilege of seeing the Promised Land. Later, Joshua led the rest of them into the land of Canaan and demanded a promise from the people that they will put away strange gods from among them and serve the LORD. Then, all the people said to Joshua saying that they chose the LORD to serve him.

"And the people said unto Joshua, The LORD our God will we serve, and

Leslie M. John

his voice will we obey". (Joshua 24:24)

**Believe in the Lord and he will supply all your needs according to His riches in glory by Christ Jesus.**

**But my God shall supply all your need according to his riches in glory by Christ Jesus. (Philippians 4:19)**

Leslie M. John

# CHAPTER 13
# DEATH DEFEATED

**M**an has an unflinching curiosity to know about the power of death, the death, and the life after death. There are many myths about the death and even among Christians there are differing views. Bible gives a believer in Christ great comfort that he or she will be with the Lord for ever and ever after death. The life after death is extremely pleasant and good according to Scriptures and, therefore, a believer in Christ does not need to be afraid of death. Lord Jesus Christ defeated the power of death and the death once and for all by His own resurrection. The grave could not hold him and He resurrected without seeing any corruption of His body.

Jesus said He had the power to lay down His life and take it back at his own discretion and He did so. Lord Jesus Christ also assured his followers that they need not be afraid of death because He gives them everlasting life. According to Bible Lord Jesus Christ is the only one who has the authority to pardon sins of a person, and salvation is by grace through faith in Him. Jesus is the Son of God, and the very God Himself. Jesus became one like us and came to this earth, lived like a man among us. Jesus was fully divine and fully human and this truth is very hard to understand by an unbeliever. Jesus died, rose on the third day and ascended into heaven. He is seated at the right hand of the Father highly exalted. He is given the name above all names and every knee shall bow to Him. Jesus will come again soon.

## THE POWER OF DEATH

God commanded the man saying to him that he may freely eat of every tree of the garden but shall not eat of the tree of the knowledge of good and evil. The wages of transgression of God's command was that he shall surely die in the day he eats thereof. (Genesis 2:16-17). God made woman out of one of the ribs of man and she became man's wife. Adam

Leslie M. John

and Eve lived happily until sin entered their lives through the deception by serpent who enticed Eve to eat from the forbidden tree. She not only ate the fruit from the forbidden tree but she gave it to man also and thus they became enemies to God. Later God visited them and pronounced punishments on Serpent, Adam and Eve. Serpent was cursed and the ground was cursed for man and God said that woman will bear children in pain. God clothed Adam and Eve with coats of skin signifying that God made a way for their reconciliation (Genesis 3:1-21).

It was when Adam and Eve sinned that Satan gained power over death and death remained in his domain. It is evident from the words of Jesus that Satan has his own kingdom and demons are as his followers. (Cf. Matthew 12:24-27)

## JESUS CALLED SATAN AS MURDERER

"Ye are of your father the devil, and the lusts of your father ye will do. He was a murderer from the beginning, and abode not in the truth, because there is no truth in him. When he speaketh a lie, he speaketh of his own: for he is a liar, and the father of it". (John 8:44)

Before the Mosaic Law was given Adam he transgressed. Cain killed Abel. Wickedness prevailed during Noah's period and Lot's period. God did not allow them to go without penalty but punished them. Apostle Paul wrote in Romans Chapter 5 about sin and death.

"Wherefore, as by one man sin entered into the world, and death by sin; and so death passed upon all men, for that all have sinned: (For until the law sin was in the world: but sin is not imputed when there is no law. Nevertheless death reigned from Adam to Moses, even over them that had not sinned after the similitude of Adam's transgression, who is the figure of him that was to come. But not as the offence, so also is the free gift. For if through the offence of one many be dead, much more the grace of God, and the gift by grace, which is by one man, Jesus Christ, hath abounded unto many. And not as it was by one that sinned, so is the gift: for the judgment was by one to condemnation, but the free gift is of many offences unto justification. For if by one man's offence death

Leslie M. John

reigned by one; much more they which receive abundance of grace and of the gift of righteousness shall reign in life by one, Jesus Christ.)" (Romans 5:12-17, Cf. also Romans 6:23)

Notice the phrase "nevertheless death reigned from Adam to Moses..." The death had power on man even before the written law was given.

"Whosoever committeth sin transgresseth also the law: for sin is the transgression of the law". (1 John 3:4)

The transgression of law is sin. Does it mean that it is applicable only from the time Mosaic Law was given? No. God's law prevailed even before the written law was given. Man was governed under Conscience and God punished sin even before the written law was given. The death reigned from Adam to Moses even when there was no written law, and death continued to have its power on sinner.

## THE STING OF DEATH

"O death, where is thy sting? O grave, where is thy victory?" (1 Corinthians 15:55)

Death has sting that hurts man and Sin causes death but that death is defeated by Jesus. In other words Satan, who is the author of sin, has the power to cause the death of a sinner. If we are without Sin, then death has no power over us; but Scripture says all have sinned and come short of the glory of God. If we say have not sinned we are liars and we make God a liar.

"For all have sinned and short of the glory of God (Romans 3:23) "If we say that we have not sinned, we make him a liar, and his word is not in us". (1 John 1:10)

The Scripture says that we shall not all sleep, but we shall all be changed. When Lazarus was dead for four days Jesus saw him and said "Our friend Lazarus sleepeth..." The disciples of Jesus took his saying at face value

Leslie M. John

and thought Lazarus was, indeed, sleeping. However, Jesus spoke of the death of Lazarus and said he is dead. Jesus said that He will wake him up from his sleep, indicating that He will raise Lazarus. Martha believed and said to Jesus that she knew Lazarus would rise in the resurrection at the last day. But then, Jesus said He is the resurrection.(Cf. John: 11:13, 14, 24 ,25)

"Jesus said unto her, I am the resurrection, and the life: he that believeth in me, though he were dead, yet shall he live" (John 11:25)

The departure of Lazarus from this earth was painful to Mary and Martha, who were sisters of Lazarus. How comforting it is to note that Jesus shares the grief of his followers and redeems them from their grief. Jesus was their good friend and shared their grief

"Jesus wept". (John 11:35)

Jesus raised Lazarus from his death and this was after four days had lapsed after his death. Many Jews believed in Jesus and some of them left that place to tell Pharisees about the resurrection of Lazarus that they saw. However, the resurrection of believers in Christ, when Christ shall come again is different from the resurrection of Lazarus, who was raised to console Mary and Martha and this miracle was one of the many miracles that Jesus did during his public ministry on this earth.

God can extend the life of a person on this earth at his discretion. Hezekiah's life was extended by fifteen years when he prayed; but there came a day when he died. (2 Kings 20:6, 2 Kings 20:21. Isaiah 38:5).

The resurrection of believers in Christ when Christ shall come again will be in the changing of corruptible bodies to incorruptible bodies in the twinkling of an eye. Apostle Paul described it in 1 Corinthians 15:51-57 where he wrote that it was a mystery that was revealed. He wrote that we shall not all sleep but will be changed and in a moment, in the twinkling of an eye, at the last trump, when our corruptible bodies will put on incorruptible bodies and rise to immortality.

Leslie M. John

The sting of death, which is sin, and the strength of sin, which is the law, puts man to death, but the death is swallowed up in victory for the believers in Christ. God gives victory over death through Lord Jesus Christ. It is in this context that he said: "O death, where is thy sting? O grave, where is thy victory?" (1 Corinthians 15:55)

There is salvation to rise from death to everlasting life. It is by confessing our sins to Jesus and by accepting Him as our personal savior. The strength of sin is the law, which points our guilt, but does not save us from Sin. It is only the blood of Lord Jesus Christ us that can cleanse us from our Sin. It is only by grace through faith in Jesus that we are saved and not by any good works. Jesus forgives us of our sins and trespasses no matter how grave they are.

When Jesus was on this earth he never saw any one die in his presence. He saw the dead and He raised them to life. Lazarus was raised to life. This is simply because Jesus is not the author of death, but of life and He gives everlasting life. God punished man when he transgressed God's command and from then onward the death reigned. The death reigned from Adam to Moses even when there was no written law because man was under the dispensation of Conscience. Satan cannot take the life of anyone who is righteous before God. Satan asked permission to end the life of Job but God denied permission to Satan while at the same time God granted him power to torment Job.

"And the LORD said unto Satan, Behold, he is in thine hand; but save his life". (Job 2:6)

As per the prophecy in Genesis 3:15, which says God has put enmity between the serpent and the woman, the serpent is given the power to bruise the heel of the seed of the woman but then the seed of the woman is given the power to bruise the head of Satan. This prophecy is about Jesus bruising the head of Satan and, indeed, Lord Jesus Christ defeated Satan at the Cross.

## DIFFERNCE BETWEEN 'KILL' AND 'MURDER'

Leslie M. John

Did God kill anyone? Yes, He killed men in the Old Testament period for reasons of disobedience or dishonoring Him. God killed many in the flood during Noah's period. He did it with fire to destroy Sodom and Gomorrah. He killed the first born of Egyptians and killed Pharaoh's army in the Red Sea. He smote Sihon the king of Amorites and killed Og, the king of Bashaan by the sword of Israel under the leadership of Moses. He killed Mighty Philistine giant Goliath by the stone from the sling of David, the shepherd.

Another classic example is in Leviticus 10:1-2 where there is a narration of the death of two sons of Aaron, who dishonored God in their pride.

"And Nadab and Abihu, the sons of Aaron, took either of them his censer, and put fire therein, and put incense thereon, and offered strange fire before the LORD, which he commanded them not. And there went out fire from the LORD, and devoured them, and they died before the LORD".

In the New Testament we see that God killed Ananias and Sapphira for deceiving Holy Spirit in addition to Judas Iscariot who committed suicide after betraying Jesus. (Acts 5:5, Acts 1:16-18)

In all this we see that God killed not only the enemies of children of Israel but He also killed those who dishonored God from among His own followers

In the Old Testament Hebrew Strong's number 5221 is transliterated as "Nakah".
In the New Testament Greek Strong's number 5407 is transliterated as "Phoneuo"

The word "Kill" means: to deprive of life, animal or vegetable, in any manner or by any means.

In the Old Testament "Murder" is translated word from Hebrew Strong's number 2026, which was transliterated as "harag"
In the New Testament "Murder" is translated word from Greek Strong's

Leslie M. John

number 5407 is transliterated as "Phoneuo"

"MUR'DER" means: the act of unlawfully killing a human being with premeditated malice, by a person of sound mind. To constitute murder in law, the person killing another must be of sound mind or in possession of his reason, and the act must be done with malice contemplated beforehand, aforethought or premeditated; but malice may be implied, as well as express.

There is not even a single verse in the Bible which says that God murdered anybody.

## ROLE OF SATAN IN THE DEATH OF JESUS

Satan is the ruler of this evil world and filled this earth sin. Satan knew that Jesus was the Son of God and, therefore, his prime aim was first to ask Him to worship Satan and thereafter murder Him. Satan tempted Jesus in the wilderness enticing Him with worldly wealth and power but Jesus did not yield to Satan's temptation. Jesus said to Satan to worship God (Matthew 4:1-11). If Satan knew that the death and resurrection of Jesus would bring salvation to mankind he would never have played a role in the death of Jesus. Satan was working towards the death of Jesus right from the time when Jesus was born in this world. Satan's aim was to defeat Jesus by asking him to worship him, in which case Satan would have had dominion over the Son of God but that did not happen . Satan took control of Herod's mind and asked the wise men to get him information about Jesus. Satan's plan through Herod was to murder Jesus, but Satan failed there. (Cf. Matthew 2:1-8)

Satan made attempts to kill Jesus though Pharisees by stoning him to death but Jesus escaped from death (Cf. John 8:59 and John 10:39). When it was time for Jesus to lay down His life, He laid it down for our sake, and He took back His life when it was time for Him to do so. Jesus had the authority over His own life, death and resurrection. It is Jesus who has the authority over our lives, death and resurrection. Satan cannot take our lives nor can hold up in the grave by his authority. Satan is given the power to end the life of a person only under the permission

Leslie M. John

from God. The life span of any person is not controlled by Satan, but it is controlled by God.

Satan had no power to take the life of Jesus because He was sinless. Satan made unlawful attempts to end the life of Jesus and lost his own right to rule over the death. Satan took possession of Judas Iscariot, a disciple of Jesus, and made him to betray Jesus, not surely with the purpose of making provision of salvation to mankind but to remove him from this earth which would pave way for him to continue to deceive man.

The death of Jesus was prophesied in Isaiah 53 and it pleased the Father to bruise Him for our sake. By the death of Jesus on the Cross for our sake, and by his burial, and by His resurrection without his body getting corrupted the death was defeated and thus Satan is defeated. This paved the way for mankind to seek salvation through grace by faith in Lord Jesus Christ. The death could not hold Jesus in the grave but Jesus rose from the dead on the third day. In John 10:17 Jesus emphatically stated that He lays down His life that He might take it again and, therefore, the Father loves him.

"Therefore doth my Father love me, because I lay down my life, that I might take it again". (John 10:17)

Lord Jesus Christ thought it not robbery to be equal with God, but He took the form of a servant and was made likeness of men. He made himself of no reputation and humbled himself and became obedient unto death, even the most wretched death on the Cross. It is because Jesus, the Son of God, who was manifest in flesh, humbled Himself so much that He was exalted by God and exalted Him. Jesus was given a name that is above every name and every knee shall bow to him. The authority of Jesus is over every thing in heaven, every thing in earth and every thing under earth (Cf. Philippians 2:6-10).

## OUR HOPE IN JESUS

Instead of taking on him the nature of angels, Jesus took on him the

Leslie M. John

form of servant in the likeness of man, of the seed of Abraham and of David, in order that he might destroy the power of death, which is the devil. The death, which had sting to hurt men and the sin that caused death, which reigned from Adam to Moses, and would have continued if Jesus did not die for the salvation of men, was defeated at the cross. The devil is defeated and the power of death is destroyed, thus rendering Satan with no power over believers in Christ. In the death and resurrection of Jesus there was a way made for the deliverance of them that were subject to the fear of death in their entire lifetime.

"Forasmuch then as the children are partakers of flesh and blood, he also himself likewise took part of the same; that through death he might destroy him that had the power of death, that is, the devil; And deliver them who through fear of death were all their lifetime subject to bondage. For verily he took not on him the nature of angels; but he took on him the seed of Abraham". (Hebrews 2:14-16)

As Jesus had promised He laid down His life for the sake of sinners that they may believe in Him and be saved and He took it back in His resurrection. In Revelation 1:18 Jesus said...

"I am he that liveth, and was dead; and, behold, I am alive for evermore, Amen; and have the keys of hell and of death"

Jesus holds the key to the hell and death and no one can put any one in hell or subject one to death without the permission from Lord Jesus Christ, who holds the key to the hell and death. However, the question is whether it is Jesus or not who takes the life of a person; be it of believer or unbeliever. No, Jesus does not take the life of any person. God did not create any one to die. Causing death was not His purpose but He punished mankind with death for sinning. It is by transgression of God's command that man was punished unto death.

Satan cannot end the life of a believer in Christ and the life of a believer in Christ does not end at any time, but it continues beyond the death. The death is only a temporary transition from earthly life to eternal life for a believer in Christ and the believer in Christ lives for ever and ever

Leslie M. John

with Lord Jesus Christ. The death is cessation of this earthly life and a fully unconscious state for an unbeliever in Christ until he is resurrected at the end for judgment and damnation in 'lake of fire' for ever and ever. Death of believer should not be compared with that of unbeliever to say that the death is cessation of life for all.

The first evidence that the soul of a believer in Christ shall not lie dead in the grave is seen in the words of none other than our Savior Lord Jesus Christ, who said to the repentant thief that he will be with the Lord in paradise the same day. The prophecy of crucifixion of Jesus and that he will be numbered along with two transgressors was recorded in Isaiah 53:12. Rightly so, when Jesus was crucified two thieves were also crucified on his either side. While one of the two thieves mocked Jesus another prayed to Jesus to remember him when He comes in His kingdom but the thief who repented before the Lord he was promised of his presence with the Lord Himself.

"And Jesus said unto him, Verily I say unto thee, To day shalt thou be with me in paradise". (Luke 23:43)

Apostle Paul wrote that when our bodies groan and are laid to be decayed in the dust our soul will be with the Lord and at the first resurrection we will rise to meet the Lord in the air. It is this great hope that a believer in Christ has that his soul will not perish but will be with the Lord Jesus Christ for ever and ever.

"For we know that if our earthly house of this tabernacle were dissolved, we have a building of God, an house not made with hands, eternal in the heavens" (2 Corinthians 5:1)
"We are confident, I say, and willing rather to be absent from the body, and to be present with the Lord". (2 Corinthians 5:8)

Those believers in Christ who have gone before us will rise first to be with the Lord for ever and ever and those that are alive when the Lord shall come with a shout, with the voice of the archangel, and with the trump of God, will be caught up to meet the Lord in the air to be with Him for ever and ever. The sinner will rise to be judged and condemned

Page 182

Leslie M. John

and will be cast into 'lake of fire' along with Satan and his fallen angels where there is gnashing of teeth and torment for ever and ever.

"For the Lord himself shall descend from heaven with a shout, with the voice of the archangel, and with the trump of God: and the dead in Christ shall rise first: Then we which are alive and remain shall be caught up together with them in the clouds, to meet the Lord in the air: and so shall we ever be with the Lord". (1 Thessalonians 4:16-17)

Leslie M. John

# CHAPTER 14
# ABRAHAM'S FAITH

It indeed takes great deal of faith and courage to trust in God. Abraham believed God without raising any doubt. God promised Abraham blessings. Abraham moved from place to place honoring God. Abram obeyed God and did everything just as God told him to do. In all these Abram believed God without any doubt and it was counted to him as righteousness.

Abram did not need to do anything other than trusting in God and go ahead in the paths ordered by God, and he obeyed God with faith. God honored his faith.

The faith Abram had on God, his obedience and honoring God need to be taken note of to see if we have such unflinching faith in God and obey him honoring him. In the New Testament as Apostle Paul and Stephen relate to the faith of Abram, who was later called "Abraham" by God, we clearly see the blessing of Abraham that we are bestowed with.

God said to Abram that in him all nations will be blessed. This blessing was given to him before the Mosaic Law came into existence. Moses came many years later, and had the blessings and covenants from God of Israel. What is interesting is that even before Israel was blessed with blessings and covenants Abram was blessed and in him all nations were blessed.

It was Abraham's unflinching faith that fetched him the honor of being reckoned as righteous. It is that kind of faith God expects us to have that we may be counted as righteous. In addition, those who believe in Jesus are made partakers of blessings and covenants of Jews (Ephesians Ch. 3:6).

## THE BLESSING OF ABRAHAM

When we consider this we stand in awe of God and glorify His name for

Leslie M. John

blessing us with spiritual blessing inherited from Abraham. It is the promise of the Father that at the very moment we repent Holy Spirit indwells us.

Jesus said that after ascending into heaven he would send the Promise of the Father and as promised the Holy Spirit came into this world to be our Comforter.

"And, behold, I send the promise of my Father upon you: but tarry ye in the city of Jerusalem, until ye be endued with power from on high". (Luke 24:49)

This giving of the Promise of the Father was fulfilled when his disciples were waiting at Jerusalem according to the instructions Lord Jesus gave them.

And they were all filled with the Holy Ghost, and began to speak with other tongues, as the Spirit gave them utterance. (Acts 2:4)

There is no more waiting needed for receiving the Holy Spirit because He is already there among us. The moment a person repents Holy Spirit indwells him or her. Apostle Paul writes in Galatians 3:7 that those which are of faith are the children of Abraham. This was an excellent gospel preached to Abraham way before he moved from the land of heathen to Canaan. The blessing that in Abraham (the then Abram) shall all the nations will be blessed and God will justify the heathen through faith was revealed by God to Abram.

Addressing the men of Israel Peter said that the God of Abraham, and of Isaac, and of Jacob glorified his Son Jesus, who was delivered up and the men of Israel denied Jesus as their Messiah in the presence of Pilate.

Jesus was the Holy One, Just and Prince of life, who was crucified by them, but was raised from the dead by God. Peter and other disciples are witnesses to this. Peter also referred Abraham in his speech. (Acts 3:25)

Apostle Paul wrote about Abraham in Galatians 3:8

"And the scripture, foreseeing that God would justify the heathen

Leslie M. John

through faith, preached before the gospel unto Abraham, saying, In thee shall all nations be blessed"

ACKNOWLEDGEMENTS
(The Old Testament Hebrew Lexicon is Brown, Driver, Briggs, Gesenius Lexicon; this is keyed to the "Theological Word Book of the Old Testament." These files are considered public domain. The New Testament Greek Lexicon based on Thayer's and Smith's Bible Dictionary plus others; this is keyed to the large Kittel and the "Theological Dictionary of the New Testament." These files are public domain. -- -- Exposition of the Old Covenant and New Covenant is by Leslie John)

# ABRAHAM WORSHIPPED

The sacrifice offered up by Abraham was complete when he had laid Isaac, his own only begotten son, on the wood upon the altar by faith that he would be raised by God. Earlier, Abraham had asked his young men, to abide there with the ass, until he went yonder, and return to them after worshipping God.

Isaac was Abraham's only begotten son, inasmuch as, he was the promised seed, and Ishmael was a son to Abraham born of his fleshly desire, when he was known as Abram before, and his wife Sarah, who was Sarai, by name, brought Hagar unto him. This act of Abraham laying down his only begotten son, Isaac, a 'type' of Jesus Christ, was confirmed in Hebrew 11:19. This shows that God is able to raise us up from the dead just as He was able to raise Isaac from the altar, and Jesus from the dead.

Job prophesied about resurrection when he said that his redeemer lives, and that he 'shall stand at the latter day upon earth'. His faith was so great when he said that even though his skin was destroyed by worms, yet he would see God in his flesh. (Job 19:25-27)

Leslie M. John

Isaiah's prophesy (in Isaiah 26:19) reveals to us that he had confidence that he would be raised from the dead.

We, who are born-again, have great privilege of seeing our Savior face to face. Apostle Paul writes in 1 Corinthians 15:50-53 'that flesh and blood cannot inherit the kingdom of God; neither doth corruption inherit incorruption'. The dead shall rise with incorruptible body.

When Jesus comes again, not all shall die, but those living shall be 'caught up', and we shall be changed in a moment. 'In a moment, in the twinkling of an eye, at the last trump: for the trumpet shall sound'. Paul and Timothy give us great hope (Philippians 3:20-21) that our vile bodies will changed unto glorious bodies.

Pillars are the strength of monuments and on the pillars are seen inscriptions or designs that either brings to us some remembrance of those, who responsibly raised them, or help us admire their beauty. Heaven does not need any pillar to support it, but the New Jerusalem, that John saw in his vision coming down from heaven was like a bride adorned for her bridegroom. In this new Jerusalem were seen the pillars on which were written the names of those, who served the living God, and the names of who those, who they served and represented.

Some in the Church at Philadelphia (Rev 3:3-5) had not defiled their garments and they were worthy to receive blessings. God promised that he who overcomes shall walk with Him. Those that overcome stand for the living God, and they are like pillars in the temple of God, and on them are written the names, such as 'name of my God', 'name of the city of my God', which is 'new Jerusalem', and His new name. (Rev 21:2-5)

## ABRAHAM OBEYED

God said to Abram to leave the country, his relatives, his father's house and go to a land that He promised to give. God promised Abram that He

Leslie M. John

will make Abram a great nation, bless him, and make his name great and that Abram will be a blessing to others. God said that whoever blesses Abram will be blessed and whoever curses Abram will be cursed. It was a great blessing that was given to Abraham. God said to Abraham "...in thee shall all families of the earth be blessed". This is a very important blessing that should be taken note of.

Abram believed and left his country along with his cousin's son, Lot and went to Canaan. While they were passing from Siechem to the plain of Moreh, God visited them and said that that land will be given to his posterity. Abram built an altar there for God. In the course of time as there was severe famine Abram went down to Egypt (Genesis 12:1-10). After having a bad experience in Egypt with the Pharaoh, who was punished by God, Abram moved with his wife and also Lot out of Egypt into the south.

"So Abram departed, as the LORD had spoken unto him; and Lot went with him: and Abram was seventy and five years old when he departed out of Haran". (Genesis 12:4)

Abram was very rich in cattle, in silver and gold. He moved further down to the place where he built an altar earlier and called on the name of the Lord. (Genesis 13:1-4)

Leslie M. John

## OUR BLESSING IN ABRAHAM

Terah 's sons were Abram, whose name was changed by God as "Abraham", and other two sons were Nahor and Haran.

Israel came into existence from the seed of Abraham. After Jacob was named as Israel as a consequence of blessings he received his posterity was called "Israel" and all others were called "Gentiles". Many years later after Solomon's death Israel was divided into two regions. One was the "House of Israel' ruled by Jeroboam and other was 'the House of Judah' ruled by Rehoboam.

Much of what we read in the Bible, especially in the Old Testament, is all about God's dealing with Israel, the division of Israel into two, and God's promise to unite them. God did not leave Gentiles aside. In due course of time God made Gentiles partakers of the Natural Olive Tree, the description of which can read in Jeremiah Chapter 11:16-17, Romans Chapters 9-11, Ephesians Chapter 3 and Galatians Chapter 3

Lot was the son of Haran who died in the land of Ur of Chaldees, before Terah died. Abram and Nahor took them wives. Abram's wife was Sarai and Nahor's wife was Milcah, who was the daughter of Haran. Terah went from Ur of Chaldees into the land of Canaan. He took with him Abram, his son, and Lot, the son of Haran, and Sarai, his daughter-in-law (Genesis 11:27-32). Abraham's son was Isaac and Isaac's son was Jacob. Jacob and his descendants are called "Israel". Chaldees was a region where heathen lived.

## YIELD TO THE WILL OF GOD

"But when he saw the wind boisterous, he was afraid; and beginning to sink, he cried, saying, Lord, save me. And immediately Jesus stretched forth his hand, and caught him, and said unto him, O thou of little faith, wherefore didst thou doubt?" Matthew 14:30-31

Jesus sent away multitudes of men, woman and children, whom he fed with five loaves and two fishes, and moved into a desert place by ship.

Page 189

Leslie M. John

# SALVATION TO GENTILES

This was after He heard that John was beheaded. Jesus asked his disciples to go by ship to the other side of the sea and He went up onto a mountain to pray until evening. He was all alone there but the ship was in the midst of the sea, and because the strong winds blew and sea tossed with waves, Jesus went toward the ship in the night. The disciples saw Jesus walking on water and going toward them, but they feared that it was a spirit and cried.

It was then that Jesus their savior told them to be of good cheer and said it was He, who was walking toward them. Peter surprisingly said to Jesus, that if He was Jesus walking toward them, then he would want to be called by Jesus and if called he would walk on the water toward Jesus.

When Peter sought help to go near the savior, Jesus said to him, 'come down out the ship'. As Peter was making endeavors to walk toward Jesus he saw that the wind was boisterous, and he was frightened. As soon as Peter was frightened, he started sinking and, therefore, cried to Jesus saying "Lord, save me".

Jesus did not leave Peter helpless but He immediately stretched forth his hand and caught him and admonished him over his little faith. Jesus questioned Peter as to why he doubted. Peter's doubt caused fear in him and the fear in him brought failure for him but when he called on his savior to help him Jesus quickly helped him. When they came into the ship, the wind stopped. Then all those who were in the ship came and worshipped him, saying the Jesus was the Son of God.

Doubt causes fear resulting in loss of faith and loss of faith brings failure but there is hope in our Savior who will surely rescue us and give us victory. Give God a chance to work in you, rather than having alternate plans to work for yourself with your own wisdom and strength.

Leslie M. John

# CHAPTER 15
# MESSAGE OF SALVATION

By offering Himself upon the cross of Calvary, Jesus opened the way for everyone to be saved. Jesus died for our sake as atonement for our sins. He was the perfect sacrifice. Jesus saved "whosoever believeth in him should not perish, but have everlasting life". Jesus, who is righteous, declares us righteous upon our confession of our sins. Through the blood of Jesus Christ we have the redemption and the forgiveness of our sins. It pleased the Father to bruise him for sake and He did that according to his riches in Grace. Grace alone saves us. We are redeemed from our sins and have obtained forgiveness of our sins through Jesus Christ.

Jesus died upon the cross of Calvary so that we may be reconciled unto Him. There is no difference whether we are Jews or Gentiles we are all one in Christ. Jesus died for all of us, and he rose from the dead and ascended in to heaven. We, who were His enemies, are made His children. The opposition that was caused between God and Man by man's sin is reconciled once and for all by Jesus Christ dying on the cross for our sake. We are reconciled unto God through His blood that was shed upon the cross of Calvary. All that we have to do is to believe that Jesus is the Lord.

## INVITATION TO SALVATION

Today is the day of Salvation. It is your choice. Jesus Christ, who bore our sins and died for our sake, is resurrected and He is living God. He will come soon to receive the saved ones to be with Him eternally. God has his own ways of gaining men for himself. My message is a request that you may please accept Jesus Christ as your personal Savior, and as your Lord, so that you may have everlasting life just as I have gained peace through Him.

Leslie M. John

Leslie M. John

www.ingramcontent.com/pod-product-compliance
Lightning Source LLC
Chambersburg PA
CBHW060240050426
42448CB00009B/1531